# American Girl®

# Around the World

## COOKBOOK

Photography **Nicole Hill Gerulat**

weldon**owen**

# Contents

Recipes from Around the World

Pacific Ocean

North America

PAGE 24
Tex-Mex Nachos
Chocolate Pudding
Watermelon-Lime Refresher
PAGE 100
PAGE 120
PAGE 71
Atlantic Ocean
Tortilla Soup
PAGE 67
PAGE 68
Cubanos
Tortas

PAGE 89
Hawaiian Fried Rice
Hawaiian Shave Ice
PAGE 103

Arroz con Pollo
South America
Brazilian Cheese Puffs
PAGE 84
Tres Leches Cakes
PAGE 36
PAGE 117
Empanadas
PAGE 38

Sticky Toffee Pudding — PAGE 119

Swedish Meatballs — PAGE 26

Smørrebrød — PAGE 61

Black Forest Cake — PAGE 50

PAGE 49

Potato Latkes — PAGE 111

Matzoh Ball Soup

Europe

Asia

PAGE 95

PAGE 86

PAGE 79

Apple Tart — PAGE 129

Fondue — PAGE 65

Tzatziki

PAGE 72

Stir-Fry — PAGE 41

Chow Mein

Paella

Gazpacho

Pesto

Pasta Soup

Souvlaki — PAGE 33

PAGE 46

Dumplings

Bucatini — PAGE 92

Shawarma — PAGE 58

Tikka Masala — PAGE 93

Japchae

Ramen Noodle Soup — PAGE 57

Krembo

Chicken Skewers — PAGE 64

PAGE 80

Couscous — PAGE 85

Hummus — PAGE 32

Mango Lassi — PAGE 126

Tandoori Chicken Wings

Fried Rice — PAGE 83

Sushi Rolls

Pacific Ocean

PAGE 96

PAGE 54

PAGE 43

PAGE 47

Falafel — PAGE 122

Chai Milkshake

PAGE 35

Pad Thai

Banh Mi

PAGE 23

Africa

PAGE 20

PAGE 113

Spring Rolls

PAGE 29

Chicken Satay

Indian Ocean

PAGE 76

Pineapple Smoothie

PAGE 108

Australia

"Marshmallow" Pudding

PAGE 127

PAGE 104

Kiwi & Berry Pavlovas

# Go on a Global Food Tour!

If you could take a trip anywhere in the world, where would you go? To Sweden, where you could try true Swedish meatballs? Or to Japan, so you could taste authentic ramen noodle soup? There are so many exciting flavors to explore on this planet! This book is dedicated to foods from all over the globe, from delicious Italian pasta dishes to time-tested Middle Eastern favorites.

In these pages, you'll find more than fifty awesome international recipes for super-fun party foods, satisfying snacks, easy weeknight dinners, and delicious desserts. Hosting a get-together? Cheese fondue, Tex-Mex nachos, and chicken satay with peanut sauce are always crowd-pleasers. Want to experiment with new ingredients? Try Vietnamese spring rolls, tandoori chicken wings, or pad thai. Craving something sweet? French apple tart, chai milkshakes, or Mexican chocolate pudding will do the trick. What's more, throughout the book, you'll find useful tips about cooking with different spices and seasonings, as well as helpful notes that offer ideas for tasty new things to try.

With these recipes as your tour guide, you can make everyday meals that taste exotic and exciting—and you may even discover your new favorite food! So get your passport ready and prepare to cook your way around the world!

# Be adventurous

Whether your family and friends call you a cooking pro or preparing a dish in this book will be your first kitchen adventure, you'll find plenty of recipes here suited to your skill level. The first chapter covers snacks and small plates so you can try your hand at fun finger foods and easy starters. From there, you'll learn how to make an array of classic soups and interesting sandwiches, some of which are perfectly portable for school. Once you've had some practice cooking with new ingredients and different spices, you'll be able to move on to more involved dishes that feature rice and noodles—they aren't necessarily more difficult, they just require a little more time and planning. And don't forget drinks and dessert! With a collection of mouthwatering sips and sweets, you can add a final touch that will make your meals memorable. Before you know it, you'll be the best cook on the planet!

# Cooking with care

 This symbol appears throughout the book to remind you that you'll need an adult to help you with all or part of the recipe. Ask for help before continuing.

Adults have lots of culinary wisdom, and they can help keep you safe in the kitchen. Always have an adult assist you, especially if your recipe involves high heat, sharp objects, and electric appliances. Be sure to wash your hands before you begin cooking and after touching raw meat, poultry, eggs, or seafood.

**Teamwork**
Adults can lend a hand when you try a new recipe, and help you stay safe when using knives and heat.

# Tip-top cooking tips

### STAY ORGANIZED

Staying organized and paying attention are important cooking skills. Before you fire up the stovetop or oven, read the recipe, including the ingredient list, from start to finish. Then it's time to clear a clean surface and lay out all of your ingredients and tools. Once the food starts cooking, don't forget to set a timer!

### GET HELP WITH SHARP TOOLS AND APPLIANCES

Make sure an adult helps you choose the correct knife for the task and that you're holding the handle firmly. When you're not using it, place it somewhere safe so it can't fall on the floor or be reached by younger siblings. Also have an adult assist you when using an electric mixer, blender, food processor, or other electric appliances, and keep them unplugged except when in use.

### WATCH THE HEAT

Stovetop burners, hot ovens, boiling water—there's a lot of heat involved in cooking, so it's important to be very careful. Always use oven mitts when handling hot equipment, and have an adult help you when you're cooking at the stovetop, moving things in and out of the oven, and working with hot liquids or foods.

# Cooking prep

You'll be able to whip up many of the recipes in this book in a snap, such as Simple Fried Rice (page 83) and Tzatziki with Pita Triangles (page 33), while others will take more time to prepare, like Japchae (page 79) and Beef Empanadas (page 38). Trying a different dish from around the world every day is totally doable when you plan ahead. Here are some thoughts to keep in mind.

### ★ PLAN AHEAD ★

Sometimes doing a little planning the day before goes a long way. Read the recipe you've chosen, make a grocery list, and go shopping with an adult to make sure that you have all the ingredients you need. Also, think about how much time you'll have to spend in the kitchen. Quick and easy noodle dishes, such as Pad Thai (page 76) and Pasta with Pesto (page 92), are great for busy weeknight dinners, while making desserts that involve a few steps, like Krembo (page 122), is an ideal weekend activity.

### ★ INVITE FRIENDS ★

Tasting new foods is fun, but trying new recipes with friends is even better! After school or on weekends, you and your co-chefs can work together to experiment with new ingredients, exotic spices, and different cuisines. It beats cooking solo!

### ★ MAKE IT SPECIAL ★

Who doesn't love a party filled with lots of delicious food and drinks? With an adult's assistance, you can throw an awesome around-the-world bash featuring dishes from all over the globe! Create a menu that includes recipes from a few different countries and add some festive decorations, such as flag bunting or travel-themed table decorations, for extra international flair.

# Small Plates
# & Snacks

# Bite-Size Falafel

Falafel, a favorite food of the Middle East, are fried balls or patties of ground chickpeas mixed with onion, garlic, and other seasonings. Serve them with yogurt-tahini sauce (see box) as a snack, or inside pita halves with shredded lettuce and diced tomato.

**MAKES 4 SERVINGS**

**2 (15-ounce) cans chickpeas, drained and rinsed**

**1 yellow onion, chopped**

**3 cloves garlic, chopped**

**1 cup packed fresh flat-leaf parsley leaves**

**2 tablespoons all-purpose flour**

**1 teaspoon baking powder**

**1 teaspoon ground cumin**

**¾ teaspoon salt**

**½ teaspoon red pepper flakes (optional)**

**Canola oil, for deep-frying**

In a food processor, combine the chickpeas, onion, garlic, and parsley and process until coarsely puréed, about 30 seconds. Transfer the mixture to a bowl and stir in the flour, baking powder, cumin, salt, and red pepper flakes, if using. Cover and refrigerate until cold, about 1 hour.

With wet hands, shape small handfuls of the chilled chickpea mixture into 1-inch round balls and set them on a large plate; you should have 12 to 14 balls.

Line a second large plate with paper towels and set the plate near the stove. Pour oil to a depth of 2 inches into a deep-fryer or large, heavy-bottomed saucepan and warm over medium-high heat until the oil registers 360°F on a deep-frying thermometer. Using tongs, carefully transfer half the balls to the hot oil. Deep-fry until golden brown on the first side, about 2 minutes. Using tongs, turn each ball and fry until golden brown on the second side, about 2 minutes longer. Using tongs, transfer the falafel to the prepared plate. Fry the remaining falafel in the same way. Serve warm with yogurt-tahini sauce.

## Yogurt-Tahini Sauce

In a small bowl, stir together ¾ cup plain yogurt; 2 tablespoons tahini; 1 clove garlic, minced; and 1 tablespoon fresh lemon juice. Taste and add as much salt and pepper as you like.

# Vietnamese Veggie Spring Rolls

These fun-to-make finger foods are perfect for a warm-weather bash. Change up the fillings as you like, and serve them with peanut sauce for dipping. Look for rice-paper wrappers and rice vermicelli in the Asian foods aisle of the grocery store.

**MAKES 12 ROLLS**

**2 teaspoons canola oil**

**1 clove garlic, minced**

**8 ounces shiitake or cremini mushrooms, stems removed, caps thinly sliced**

**1 teaspoon low-sodium soy sauce**

**7 ounces dried rice vermicelli**

**12 (8½-inch) rice-paper wrappers**

**1 red bell pepper, seeded and thinly sliced**

**2 ripe avocados, pitted, peeled, and sliced**

**2 carrots, peeled and shredded**

**1 cup mixed fresh mint leaves, basil leaves, and cilantro sprigs**

**Peanut Sauce (page 29), for serving**

Put 1½ teaspoons of the canola oil in a large nonstick frying pan and set the pan over medium-high heat. Add the garlic and cook, stirring constantly, until fragrant but not browned, about 30 seconds. Add the mushrooms and cook, stirring occasionally, until they release their moisture, 3 to 4 minutes. Add the soy sauce and cook until the pan is dry, about 1 minute. Transfer to a bowl and set aside.

Fill a large pot three-fourths full of water. Set the pot over high heat and bring the water to a boil. Add the rice vermicelli, stir to separate, and cook until tender, 3 to 5 minutes, or according to the package directions. Drain the noodles in a colander and rinse under cold running water. Return the noodles to the pot, drizzle with the remaining ½ teaspoon canola oil, and toss to coat.

Fill a pie plate with very hot tap water. Soak a rice-paper wrapper in the water until flexible, about 30 seconds. Lift the wrapper out of the water and lay the wrapper on a clean work surface. Arrange a combination of noodles, bell pepper slices, avocado slices, mushrooms, carrot shreds, and herbs across the center of the wrapper, keeping about 1½ inches free on the left and right sides. Fold the left and right ends over the fillings. Starting from the edge closest to you, tightly roll the wrapper, enclosing the fillings. Set the spring roll aside. Repeat with the remaining wrappers and fillings.

Cut each roll in half diagonally, arrange on a platter, and serve with the peanut sauce.

# Tex-Mex Chicken & Black Bean Nachos

These awesome nachos are a great snack, but they're so hearty you can even enjoy them for lunch or dinner. With protein from the chicken and beans and a healthy topping of fresh tomatoes and avocado, this dish is as good for you as it is scrumptious!

**MAKES 4 TO 6 SERVINGS**

**2 teaspoons ground cumin**

**2 teaspoons chili powder**

**½ teaspoon salt**

**3 small boneless, skinless chicken breast halves**

**2 teaspoons canola oil**

**3 cups corn tortilla chips**

**2 (15-ounce) cans black beans, rinsed and drained**

**6 ounces shredded Monterey jack cheese**

**2 ripe tomatoes, diced**

**1 ripe avocado, pitted, peeled, and cut into ½-inch cubes**

**½ cup sour cream**

 Preheat the oven to 375°F. Line a rimmed cookie sheet with aluminum foil.

In a small bowl, stir together the cumin, chili powder, and salt. Lay the chicken on the prepared cookie sheet, brush on both sides with the canola oil, and sprinkle with the spice mixture. Bake until the thickest part of the chicken is no longer pink when cut into with a paring knife, about 25 minutes. Remove from the oven and let cool. When the chicken is cool enough to handle, using your fingers or 2 forks, shred the meat into bite-sized pieces.

Position an oven rack about 6 inches from the upper heating element and preheat the broiler.

Spread the tortilla chips in an even layer on a large cast-iron pan or clean rimmed cookie sheet. Top them with the black beans, followed by the shredded chicken and then the cheese. Carefully place the cookie sheet under the broiler and broil just until the cheese is melted, about 3 minutes. Some broilers are much hotter than others, so keep a close watch!

Remove the pan from the broiler. Using a large, wide spatula, carefully transfer the nachos to a serving platter. (If baking the nachos in a cast-iron pan, you can serve them directly from the pan, if you like.) Sprinkle the diced tomatoes and avocado cubes on top and dollop with the sour cream. Serve right away.

# Swedish Meatballs

You just can't go wrong with tender, lightly spiced meatballs in a rich, creamy sauce. The traditional garnish for Swedish meatballs is lingonberry jam, but if you have trouble finding some, use cranberry sauce or red currant or raspberry preserves instead.

**MAKES ABOUT 42 MEATBALLS**

**MEATBALLS**

**3 tablespoons unsalted butter**

**½ yellow onion, finely chopped**

**Salt**

**1 cup fresh white bread crumbs**

**¼ cup whole milk**

**2 large eggs, lightly beaten**

**½ teaspoon ground nutmeg**

**½ teaspoon ground cardamom**

**1 pound ground beef**

**1 pound ground pork**

**3 tablespoons olive oil**

To make the meatballs, put 1 tablespoon of the butter in a large nonstick frying pan and set the pan over medium heat. When the butter is melted, add the onion and a pinch of salt and cook, stirring often, until tender and translucent, about 5 minutes. Remove the pan from the heat.

In a large bowl, combine the bread crumbs and milk and stir with a wooden spoon until evenly moistened. Add the eggs, 1 teaspoon salt, nutmeg, cardamom, and the cooked onion and stir well. Add the beef and pork and mix gently with the spoon or your hands until the ingredients are well combined. Using your hands, shape the mixture into 1-inch balls and set them on a rimmed cookie sheet. Wipe out the frying pan.

Line a large plate with paper towels and set the plate near the stove. Put the remaining 2 tablespoons butter and the olive oil in the same frying pan, set the pan over medium-high heat, and let heat for 2 minutes. Add as many meatballs as will comfortably fit in the pan (don't crowd them in) and cook, turning them 3 or 4 times, until browned on all sides, about 10 minutes total. Transfer the meatballs to the prepared plate. Repeat with the remaining meatballs. After all of the meatballs have been browned, use a rubber spatula to scrape the fat and any bits in the pan into a bowl and discard. Wipe out the pan.

## Dinnertime!

*To make this dish into a meal, serve it over buttered egg noodles or mashed potatoes.*

**SAUCE**

¼ cup (½ stick) unsalted butter

¼ cup all-purpose flour

2 cups beef broth

Salt and ground black pepper

¾ cup sour cream

Chopped fresh chives or flat-leaf parsley leaves, for garnish (optional)

Lingonberry jam, cranberry sauce, or red currant or raspberry preserves, for serving

To make the sauce, put the butter in the same frying pan and set the pan over medium heat. Sprinkle the flour over the butter, whisk to combine, and cook for about 1 minute, stirring constantly. While whisking, slowly add the beef broth and bring to a simmer, stirring often. Taste the sauce (careful, it's hot!) and season with as much salt and pepper as you like.

Carefully return the meatballs to the pan. Cover, reduce the heat to low, and simmer, stirring occasionally, until the meatballs are cooked through, about 10 minutes. Add the sour cream, stir to combine, and cook just until the sauce is warmed through, 1 to 2 minutes.

Transfer the meatballs and sauce to a serving bowl. Garnish with chives or parsley (if using) and serve right away, passing jam at the table.

# Chicken Satay with Peanut Sauce

Satay, or grilled marinated meat on skewers, is typically sold as a snack by street vendors in Indonesia, Malaysia, Singapore, and Thailand. Here in the States, it's a popular appetizer in Southeast Asian restaurants. This recipe is perfect for a party.

**MAKES 8 SERVINGS**

**SATAY**

1 cup coconut milk

¼ cup fish sauce

4 cloves garlic, finely chopped

¼ cup chopped fresh cilantro

1 teaspoon curry powder

1 teaspoon ground black pepper

8 medium boneless, skinless chicken breast halves, cut crosswise into ½-inch strips

Canola oil, for greasing the pan

**PEANUT SAUCE**

½ cup smooth peanut butter

Juice of 1 lime

1 tablespoon low-sodium soy sauce

1 tablespoon firmly packed light brown sugar

To prepare the satay, in a medium bowl, stir together the coconut milk, fish sauce, garlic, cilantro, curry powder, and pepper. Put the chicken in a large zipper-lock bag and pour in the coconut milk mixture. Seal the bag and gently massage to make sure the chicken is evenly coated with the marinade. Refrigerate for at least 4 hours or up to 8 hours.

Line a cookie sheet with paper towels. Remove the chicken from the marinade, lay the chicken strips on the prepared cookie sheet, and pat dry with additional paper towels. Set the chicken aside. Discard the marinade.

To make the peanut sauce, in a small bowl, stir together the peanut butter, lime juice, soy sauce, and brown sugar until the sugar dissolves. Add water to thin the sauce, if you like. Transfer to a serving bowl and set aside.

Thread the chicken strips lengthwise onto sixteen 6-inch wooden or metal skewers, dividing them evenly.

Set a nonstick grill pan over medium-high heat and let heat for about 2 minutes. Lightly brush the grill pan with canola oil. Place as many skewers as will comfortably fit in the grill pan (don't crowd them in) and cook, turning once with tongs, until the chicken is nicely grill-marked on both sides, about 4 minutes per side. Transfer to a platter and repeat to cook the remaining chicken, lightly brushing the pan with additional canola oil before each batch.

Serve the satay with the peanut sauce, and garnish with cilantro, if you like.

# Roasted Red Pepper Hummus

In this jazzy twist on the classic chickpea dip, roasted red pepper adds a fun orange-red color and a touch of sweetness. It's delicious spread on sandwiches and wraps or served with pita chips. Tahini, a purée of toasted sesame seeds, adds a subtle nutty flavor.

**MAKES ABOUT 1 CUP**

1 (15-ounce) can chickpeas, rinsed and drained

1 jarred roasted red bell pepper, patted dry and roughly chopped

2 tablespoons extra-virgin olive oil

2 teaspoons tahini

1 teaspoon ground cumin

½ teaspoon smoked paprika

½ teaspoon salt

Juice of 1 lemon

Pita Triangles (page 33), for serving

In a blender or food processor, combine the chickpeas, roasted bell pepper, olive oil, tahini, cumin, smoked paprika, salt, and lemon juice. Process until smooth, scraping down the blender or work bowl with a rubber spatula once or twice.

Transfer the hummus to a bowl. Serve right away with pita triangles, or refrigerate in an airtight container for up to 2 days.

# Tzatziki with Pita Triangles

Tzatziki (pronounced tsah-ZEE-kee) is a Greek dip or sauce made with tangy yogurt and cool cucumber. You can serve it as a snack with pita triangles or toasted pita bread, but it's also amazing in sandwich wraps or as a sauce for grilled chicken or fish.

**MAKES ABOUT 2 CUPS**

**PITA TRIANGLES**

**2 (6-inch) pita breads**

**Olive oil, for brushing the pita**

**Salt**

**TZATZIKI**

**1 cup plain whole-milk or Greek yogurt**

**1 cup peeled and grated English cucumber**

**1 teaspoon minced fresh mint or flat-leaf parsley**

**1 teaspoon fresh lemon juice**

**Salt**

To make the pita triangles, preheat the oven to 350°F.

Split each pita bread in half to create 4 thin rounds. Brush both sides of the rounds with olive oil. Cut each round into 8 evenly sized triangles. Spread the pita triangles in a single layer on a rimmed cookie sheet and lightly sprinkle with salt. Place the cookie sheet in the oven and toast the pita triangles, turning them once, until golden and crisp, about 10 minutes. Remove from the oven and let cool completely.

To make the tzatziki, in a medium bowl, combine the yogurt, cucumber, mint or parsley, and lemon juice and stir until well combined. Taste and add as much salt as you like.

Serve the tzatziki with the pita triangles.

# Tandoori Chicken Wings

These Indian-inspired wings pack a serious punch of flavor, but the fresh dipping sauce will cool down your taste buds. The name derives from *tandoor*, a deep, round, charcoal-fueled clay oven that gives any foods cooked in it a distinctive smoky finish.

**MAKES 4 SERVINGS**

## CHICKEN WINGS

**¾ cup plain whole-milk yogurt**

**1 tablespoon tomato paste**

**1 tablespoon fresh lemon juice**

**2 teaspoons garam masala**

**1 teaspoon ground turmeric**

**1 teaspoon salt**

**¼ teaspoon cayenne pepper**

**3 pounds chicken wings and drumettes**

**Nonstick cooking spray**

## YOGURT SAUCE

**¾ cup plain whole-milk yogurt**

**Grated zest and juice of 1 lemon**

**1 tablespoon chopped fresh cilantro**

**Salt and ground black pepper**

To make the chicken wings, in a large bowl, stir together the yogurt, tomato paste, lemon juice, garam masala, turmeric, salt, and cayenne. Add the chicken wings to the bowl and toss to coat well. Cover and refrigerate for 30 minutes.

Position an oven rack about 6 inches from the upper heating element and preheat the broiler. Line a large rimmed cookie sheet with aluminum foil and coat it lightly with nonstick cooking spray.

Remove the chicken wings from the marinade and arrange them in an even layer on the prepared cookie sheet. Place the cookie sheet under the broiler and cook for 8 minutes. Carefully remove the cookie sheet and, using tongs, flip each chicken wing. Continue to broil until the chicken is opaque throughout, about 8 minutes longer. Don't worry if some of the wings have blackened spots (that's the way tandoori chicken is meant to be). Remove from the oven and let cool on the cookie sheet on a wire rack.

To make the yogurt sauce, in a small bowl, stir together the yogurt, lemon zest and juice, and cilantro. Taste and add as much salt and pepper as you like. Transfer to a serving bowl.

Transfer the chicken wings to a platter and serve warm, with the sauce.

# Brazilian Cheese Puffs

In Brazil, these crispy and chewy gluten-free puffs are a favorite afternoon snack. They are often made with sour tapioca flour, giving them a unique flavor. But for this recipe, look for regular tapioca flour in the gluten-free section or baking aisle of your market.

**MAKES ABOUT 26 PUFFS**

**2¼ cups tapioca flour**

**¾ cup water**

**½ cup whole milk**

**¼ cup canola oil, plus more for oiling your hands**

**¾ teaspoon salt**

**2 large eggs**

**1 cup grated Parmesan cheese**

 Position 2 racks evenly spaced in the oven and preheat the oven to 425°F. Line two large rimmed cookie sheets with parchment paper.

Put the tapioca flour in the bowl of a stand mixer fitted with the paddle attachment. Combine the water, milk, canola oil, and salt in a medium saucepan. Set the pan over high heat and bring the mixture to a boil, watching carefully so that it doesn't boil over. When it reaches a boil, immediately pour it over the tapioca flour. Beat on low speed until combined, about 1 minute; the mixture will be very stiff. Stop the mixer. Crack an egg into a small bowl and, with the mixer on low speed, add the egg. Increase the speed to medium-high and beat until well combined, about 1 minute. Stop the mixer and add the second egg in the same way. Add the Parmesan and beat on medium speed until well combined. Stop the mixer, lightly oil your hands, and pat down the dough.

With lightly oiled hands or an ice cream scoop, scoop up a tablespoon of the dough and roll it into a ball between your palms. Place the ball on a prepared cookie sheet. Repeat with the remaining dough, spacing the balls about 1 inch apart on the cookie sheets. You should have about 26 balls.

Turn down the oven temperature to 350°F, quickly slide the cookie sheets into the oven, and bake for 15 minutes. Using oven mitts, carefully rotate the cookie sheets from top to bottom and front to back and bake until the cheese puffs are light golden brown, 15 to 20 minutes longer. Remove from the oven and let cool on the baking sheet on wire racks for about 5 minutes. Serve warm.

**Perfect portions**
Using an ice cream scoop with a spring is an easy way to shape the dough into equal-sized balls.

# Beef Empanadas

Savory turnovers called empanadas are popular snacks in Latin America. They're super-portable, so they're the perfect finger food for a picnic or a party. These are filled with a yummy cumin-spiced mixture of ground beef, pine nuts, and dried currants.

**MAKES ABOUT 24 EMPANADAS**

**DOUGH**

1¾ cups all-purpose flour, plus more for dusting

¼ teaspoon salt

½ cup (1 stick) cold unsalted butter, cut into ½-inch cubes

1 large egg, lightly beaten

2 tablespoons ice water

1½ teaspoons fresh lemon juice

**FILLING**

6 ounces ground beef

3 tablespoons pine nuts, coarsely chopped

½ yellow onion, finely chopped

1 tablespoon tomato paste

*(See additional ingredients, next page)*

To make the dough, put the flour, salt, and butter in a food processor and pulse a few times, or until the mixture forms coarse crumbs. In a small bowl, whisk together the egg, water, and lemon juice. With the motor running, quickly pour the egg mixture through the feed tube and process just until the dough comes together. Turn the dough out onto a lightly floured work surface and, using your hands, form it into a disk. Wrap the disk in plastic wrap and refrigerate for 30 minutes.

While the dough chills, make the filling. Put the beef and pine nuts in a large frying pan. Set the pan over medium heat and cook, stirring with a wooden spoon to break up the meat, until the beef is no longer pink, about 6 minutes. Using a slotted spoon, transfer to a medium bowl. Pour off almost all of the fat from the pan. Add the onion to the pan and cook over medium heat, stirring occasionally, until softened, about 5 minutes. Add the tomato paste and cook, stirring occasionally, until the mixture is thick and dry, about 3 minutes. Remove from the heat and add the tomato-onion mixture along with the currants, cumin, oregano, ¼ teaspoon salt, and ¼ teaspoon pepper to the beef mixture and stir to combine. Taste the mixture and add more salt and pepper, if you like.

Position 2 racks so that they are evenly spaced in the oven and preheat the oven to 375°F. Line 2 cookie sheets with parchment paper.

**Mix it up**

*The empanada filling can also be made with ground turkey, ground pork, or a combination.*

**3 tablespoons dried currants**

**½ teaspoon ground cumin**

**¼ teaspoon dried oregano**

**Salt and ground black pepper**

**1 large egg**

In a small bowl, whisk together the egg and 1 tablespoon water.

On a lightly floured work surface, use a rolling pin to roll out the chilled dough to a ¼-inch thickness. Using a 3-inch round biscuit cutter, cut out as many rounds as you can. Transfer the rounds to the prepared cookie sheets, arranging them in a single layer. Gather the dough scraps, roll them out, and cut out additional rounds. You should have about 24 rounds. Brush them with the egg mixture.

Place a generous tablespoon of filling in the center of each round. Lift the edges of each round so they meet in the center, compacting the filling and forming a fan shape. Using your fingers, firmly crimp the edges. Lay them on their sides and press the top edges with a fork to seal them completely. Brush the empanadas with the egg mixture. Bake until golden brown, about 30 minutes. Remove from the oven and let cool slightly on the cookie sheets on wire racks.

Transfer the empanadas to a platter and serve warm.

# Asian Veggie Dumplings

Who doesn't love plump dumplings with a sweet-tangy dipping sauce? These are browned in a frying pan and then steamed in the same pan, so you don't need a steamer basket. Look for wonton wrappers in the refrigerated aisle of your supermarket.

**MAKES ABOUT 28 DUMPLINGS**

## DIPPING SAUCE

¼ cup low-sodium
soy sauce

1 tablespoon rice vinegar

1 teaspoon firmly packed
light brown sugar

½ teaspoon peeled and
grated fresh ginger

¼ teaspoon toasted
sesame oil (optional)

## DUMPLINGS

2 teaspoons low-sodium
soy sauce

2 teaspoons hoisin sauce

1 teaspoon peeled and
grated fresh ginger

6 teaspoons canola oil,
plus more as needed

1 cup finely shredded
green cabbage

½ cup finely chopped
cremini mushrooms
(about 5 mushrooms)

To make the dipping sauce, in a small bowl, stir together the soy sauce, vinegar, brown sugar, ginger, and sesame oil (if using) until the sugar dissolves. Cover and set aside.

To make the dumplings, in a small bowl, stir together the soy sauce, hoisin sauce, and ginger. Put 2 teaspoons canola oil in a large nonstick frying pan, set the pan over medium heat, and let heat for 2 minutes. Add the cabbage, mushrooms, carrot, and salt and cook, stirring often, until the vegetables are slightly softened, about 3 minutes. Add the green onions and soy sauce mixture and stir to combine. Transfer to a bowl to cool to room temperature. Wipe out the pan.

Put some water in a small bowl. Spoon about ¼ cup cornstarch into a fine-mesh sieve and dust a large rimmed cookie sheet with it until covered with a thin, even layer. Lay 1 wonton wrapper on a clean work surface. Spoon 1 teaspoon of the veggie mixture in the center of the wrapper. Dip your fingers in the water and lightly moisten the edges of the wrapper. Fold the wrapper in half (if using squares, fold the wrapper in half diagonally, to form a triangle) and press the edges together to seal. Place the dumpling on the prepared cookie sheet. Repeat with additional wrappers and the remaining filling until you've used up all the filling. (At this point, you can freeze some of the dumplings in a single layer on the cookie sheet. Once they are frozen, transfer them to a zipper-lock bag and freeze for up to 3 months. Don't thaw them before cooking, but add a few minutes to the cooking time.)

~ Continued on page 42 ~

## Festive fare

*Dumplings are a tasty way to start a party. Set out a bunch of colorful chopsticks and invite friends to dig in.*

⅓ cup peeled and shredded carrot

Pinch of salt

2 green onions, thinly sliced

Cornstarch, for dusting

1 package round or square wonton wrappers

~ *Continued from page 41* ~

Brush the same frying pan with 2 teaspoons canola oil, set the pan over medium heat, and let heat for 2 minutes. Dusting off the cornstarch as you add them, place as many dumplings as will comfortably fit in a single layer in the pan (don't crowd them in) and cook until browned on the bottoms, 2 to 3 minutes. Using tongs, gently flip the dumplings. Carefully pour about ½ cup water into the pan (it will bubble and steam vigorously, so be careful), cover, and cook until the water evaporates, about 4 minutes.

Transfer the dumplings to a serving platter and cover lightly with aluminum foil to keep warm. Repeat to cook the remaining dumplings, brushing the pan with 2 teaspoons canola oil before each batch.

Serve the dumplings warm, with the dipping sauce.

# Veggie Sushi Hand Rolls

Cone-shaped sushi hand rolls, called *temaki,* are an easy way to get started making sushi. Once you get the hang of working with the ingredients, you can try assembling sushi rolls using a traditional bamboo rolling mat for a fancier finish.

MAKES 6 ROLLS

**SEASONED RICE**

2 tablespoons
rice vinegar

1½ tablespoons sugar

½ tablespoon salt

1½ cups cooked
short-grain white rice
(see Steamed Rice,
page 83), still hot

1 teaspoon rice vinegar

3 sheets nori, cut in half

1 tablespoon toasted
sesame seeds

½ English cucumber,
peeled and cut into
matchsticks

1 carrot, peeled and
cut into matchsticks

1 ripe avocado, pitted,
peeled, and thinly sliced

Low-sodium soy sauce
and pickled ginger,
for serving (optional)

To make the seasoned rice, combine the vinegar, sugar, and salt in a small saucepan. Set the pan over low heat and cook, stirring, until the sugar and salt dissolve, about 2 minutes. Let cool completely.

Put the hot cooked rice in a large baking dish and use a spatula to spread it out evenly. Slowly pour in the vinegar mixture while slicing the spatula through the rice; flip the rice with the spatula to mix in the vinegar mixture but do not stir. Cover with a clean, damp kitchen towel until ready to use.

To assemble the hand rolls, combine the vinegar with 2 tablespoons water in a small bowl. Place 1 piece of nori shiny side down on a clean, dry work surface with a long side closest to you. Scoop about 1/4 cup of seasoned rice onto the left third of the nori. Lightly moisten your fingers with the vinegar-water mixture and gently flatten the rice; don't let the rice spread too much or cover the corners. Lightly sprinkle the rice with 1/2 teaspoon sesame seeds and place a few pieces of cucumber, carrot, and avocado diagonally on the rice, angled up to the far left corner of the nori. Lift the bottom left corner of the nori, bring it up over the fillings, and begin rolling, forming a point at the bottom right edge of the rice; keep rolling until the nori forms a cone around the fillings. Very lightly moisten the seam with the vinegar-water mixture to seal it. Set the hand roll on a platter. Repeat with the remaining ingredients.

Serve the hand rolls with soy sauce and pickled ginger, if using.

Temaki

Maki

***Roll with it!***
Making sushi at home
is fun. Start with temaki
(cone-shaped hand rolls)
then try maki, traditional
rolls made with a
bamboo mat.

# Souvlaki

In Greek, *souvla* means "skewer," and meat cooked on skewers is called *souvlaki*. Lamb is the traditional meat for this dish, but if you prefer, you can use chicken breasts or pork loin instead. Serve these skewers with Tzatziki (page 33).

**MAKES 4 SERVINGS**

¼ cup fresh lemon juice

3 tablespoons extra-virgin olive oil

3 cloves garlic, minced

2 tablespoons chopped fresh flat-leaf parsley

1 large bay leaf

½ teaspoon salt

⅛ teaspoon ground black pepper

⅛ teaspoon red pepper flakes

1½ pounds boneless leg of lamb, cut into 20 cubes

1 large green bell pepper, stemmed, seeded, and cut lengthwise into 12 pieces (optional)

2 small yellow onions, each cut into 6 wedges

8 cherry tomatoes

Canola oil, for greasing the pan

In a large zipper-lock bag, combine the lemon juice, olive oil, garlic, parsley, bay leaf, salt, black pepper, and red pepper flakes. Add the lamb cubes, seal the bag, and gently massage to make sure the meat is evenly coated with the marinade. Refrigerate for at least 8 hours or up to 24 hours.

Line a large plate with paper towels. Remove the lamb from the marinade, lay the pieces on the prepared plate, and pat dry with additional paper towels. Discard the marinade. Onto each of four 12-inch wooden or metal skewers, thread 5 lamb cubes, 3 bell pepper strips (if using), 3 onion wedges, and 2 cherry tomatoes, beginning and ending with a lamb cube and alternating the ingredients.

Set a large nonstick grill pan over medium-high heat and let heat for about 2 minutes. Lightly brush the grill pan with canola oil. Place the skewers in the grill pan and cook, using tongs to turn them occasionally, until the meat is nicely grill-marked on all sides and is pink inside when cut into with a sharp knife, about 8 minutes total.

Transfer the skewers to a platter and serve right away.

# Moroccan-Spiced Chicken Skewers

Moroccan food is seasoned with lots of fragrant spices that add bold, exotic flavor to dishes like this one and fill the house with the best aromas. To turn these skewers into a Moroccan meal, serve them with Couscous with Apricots & Almonds (page 85).

**MAKES 4 SERVINGS**

**1 teaspoon salt**

**1 teaspoon ground cumin**

**1 teaspoon paprika**

**1 teaspoon ground turmeric**

**½ teaspoon ground cinnamon**

**¼ teaspoon garlic powder**

**⅛ teaspoon cayenne pepper**

**3 small boneless, skinless chicken breast halves, cut into 1-inch cubes**

**2 tablespoons olive oil**

**1 large red bell pepper, stemmed, seeded, and cut into 8 pieces**

**Canola oil, for greasing the pan**

In a small bowl, stir together the salt, cumin, paprika, turmeric, cinnamon, garlic powder, and cayenne. In a large bowl, toss the chicken with the olive oil until evenly coated. Sprinkle with the spice mixture and toss again. Thread the chicken and bell pepper pieces onto four 6-inch wooden or metal skewers, dividing them evenly and pressing them together snugly.

Set a nonstick grill pan over medium-high heat and let heat for about 2 minutes. Lightly brush the grill pan with canola oil. Place the skewers in the grill pan and cook, using tongs to turn them occasionally, until the chicken is nicely grill-marked on all sides and feels firm when pressed, 8 to 10 minutes total.

Transfer the skewers to a plate and serve right away.

# Potato Latkes

Latkes are Jewish potato pancakes that are fried until brown and crisp, and they're usually served with sour cream and applesauce for dolloping on top. Don't fuss with the latkes once they are in the pan; they need time to brown or they will fall apart.

**MAKES 4 SERVINGS**

**1 pound russet potatoes, peeled, or ½ pound each russet potatoes and sweet potatoes, peeled**

**3 large eggs, lightly beaten**

**¾ cup almond flour**

**⅓ cup minced fresh flat-leaf parsley**

**2 cloves garlic, minced**

**1 teaspoon salt**

**½ teaspoon ground black pepper**

**Unsalted butter, for frying**

**Sour cream, for serving**

**Applesauce, for serving**

Using the large holes on a box grater-shredder, shred the potatoes. In a large bowl, combine the shredded potatoes, eggs, almond flour, parsley, garlic, salt, and pepper and mix with a rubber spatula until well combined.

Preheat the oven to 200°F.

Put 1½ teaspoons butter in a medium nonstick frying pan and set the pan over medium heat. When the butter has melted, carefully swirl the pan to coat the surface with butter. Scoop up ¼ cup of the potato mixture and, using your hands, form it into a ¼-inch-thick round. Carefully place the latke in the pan and repeat to make more latkes, shaping only as many as will comfortably fit in a single layer in the pan. Cook, without pressing on or moving the latkes, until lightly browned on the bottoms, about 3 minutes. Using a wide spatula, carefully flip each latke and continue to cook until lightly browned on the second side, about 3 minutes. Transfer to a rimmed cookie sheet and keep warm in the oven. Repeat, adding more butter to the pan before cooking each batch, until you've used all of the potato mixture.

Set out sour cream and applesauce in serving bowls. Arrange the warm latkes on a platter and serve right away.

# Cheese Fondue

If you don't have a fondue pot, you can make this party-perfect appetizer in a saucepan, transfer it to a heatproof serving bowl, set the bowl over a pot of just-boiled water, and bring the pot to the table. The fondue will stay warm and gooey while everyone dips in.

**MAKES 4 TO 6 SERVINGS**

**2 cups shredded Gruyère cheese**

**2 cups shredded Emmentaler, Swiss, or fontina cheese**

**2 tablespoons cornstarch**

**½ cup low-sodium vegetable broth**

**½ cup water**

**3 tablespoons apple cider vinegar**

**1 or 2 loaves French bread, cut into 1-inch cubes, for dipping**

**1 apple, cut into thin wedges, for dipping**

**1 cup cauliflower or broccoli florets, for dipping**

Place the Gruyère and Emmentaler cheeses in a large zipper-lock bag and add the cornstarch. Seal the bag and shake until the cheeses are evenly coated with the cornstarch.

Combine the vegetable broth, water, and cider vinegar in a fondue pot or saucepan. Set the pot over medium-high heat and bring the liquid to a boil. Reduce the heat to medium. While whisking, add a handful of the cheese mixture to the pot and whisk until it is almost melted. Repeat with the remaining cheese mixture. Once you've added all of the cheese mixture, continue whisking until the mixture bubbles gently and is completely smooth, about 1 minute longer.

Carefully set the pot on its base over the heat source recommended by the manufacturer, or set the saucepan on a trivet (or over a pot of just-boiled water) on the table. Set out fondue forks. Put the bread, apple wedges, and cauliflower or broccoli florets on a platter, and serve right away.

PAS

# Soups & Sandwiches

# Veggie Banh Mi

This veggie-filled *banh mi,* or Vietnamese sandwich, packs a lot of tang and crunch in a crusty roll. For a different but equally delicious flavor, try it with thinly sliced eggplant or tofu instead of the portobello mushrooms.

**MAKES 4 SANDWICHES**

**2 carrots, peeled and shredded on the large holes of a box grater**

**½ cup thinly sliced English cucumber**

**8 thin slices from ½ sweet onion (such as Vidalia or Walla Walla)**

**½ cup rice vinegar**

**2 tablespoons sugar**

**4 tablespoons low-sodium soy sauce**

**2 tablespoons olive oil**

**4 (4-inch) portobello mushrooms, stems removed**

**4 crusty whole-grain rolls or 1 baguette cut into 4 pieces, split horizontally**

**4 tablespoons mayonnaise**

**4 tablespoons minced fresh cilantro**

Preheat the oven to 400°F.

In a medium bowl, combine the grated carrot, cucumber slices, and onion slices. Add the vinegar and sugar and stir to coat. Set aside.

In a small bowl, stir together the soy sauce and olive oil. Brush the mixture onto both sides of the mushroom caps. Place the mushrooms on a rimmed cookie sheet and roast until tender, 12 to 15 minutes. Remove from the oven and let cool. Meanwhile, turn off the oven and place the rolls or baguette pieces, cut side up, on a clean cookie sheet and toast them for 5 to 10 minutes, until they are golden brown. When the mushrooms are cool enough to handle, using a serrated knife, cut them into ½-inch slices.

In another small bowl, stir together the mayonnaise, cilantro, and 1 teaspoon of liquid from the vegetable mixture. Spread the mayonnaise on the bottom half of each roll or baguette and top with equal amounts of mushroom slices. Drain the vegetable mixture and mound it on top of the mushroom slices, dividing it evenly. Cover with the top halves of the bread and serve right away.

**Slurp, slurp!**
Most of the time, slurping your food is considered impolite. But when eating noodle soup in Japan, it's actually encouraged!

# Ramen Noodle Soup

This tasty, easy-to-make noodle soup is so much more satisfying than store-bought instant ramen. To make the dish really hearty, add soft-boiled egg halves, thin slices of roasted pork, cooked corn kernels, and/or sesame seeds to each bowl just before serving.

**MAKES 6 SERVINGS**

**4 cups low-sodium chicken broth**

**2 cups water**

**¼ cup low-sodium soy sauce**

**3 tablespoons ketchup**

**⅛ teaspoon chili oil (optional)**

**9 ounces ramen noodles**

**8 ounces shiitake, cremini, or white mushrooms, caps thinly sliced**

**½ cup cooked, shelled edamame**

**4 green onions, chopped**

**Hot sauce, such as Sriracha, for serving (optional)**

Combine the chicken broth, water, soy sauce, ketchup, and chili oil (if using) in a large pot. Set the pot over medium-high heat and bring to a boil. Add the noodles, mushrooms, and edamame. Reduce the heat to medium-low and simmer until the noodles are tender (check the package for the cooking time).

Divide the noodles and broth among 6 bowls. Sprinkle each serving with green onions and serve right away, passing the hot sauce (if using) at the table.

# Chicken Shawarma Pita Pockets

Shawarma, a Middle Eastern specialty, is seasoned meat that is slow-roasted on a big spit, and sliced thin for serving. With this recipe, you can make a version of shawarma at home by grilling strips of marinated chicken and then tucking them into pita bread.

**MAKES 6 SERVINGS**

**2 tablespoons olive oil**

**2 teaspoons curry powder**

**1 teaspoon ground cumin**

**2 cloves garlic, minced**

**Juice of ½ lemon**

**Salt and ground black pepper**

**4 boneless, skinless chicken breast halves, cut crosswise into ½-inch-thick strips**

**1 red onion, halved and cut into ½-inch half-moons**

**3 pita breads, halved**

**6 to 8 romaine lettuce leaves, torn to fit inside pitas**

**2 ripe plum tomatoes, thinly sliced**

**Yogurt-Tahini Sauce (page 20), for serving**

In a large bowl, stir together 1 tablespoon of the olive oil, the curry powder, cumin, garlic, lemon juice, 1 teaspoon salt, and ¼ teaspoon pepper. Add the chicken and toss until well coated. Let stand at room temperature for 20 minutes.

Meanwhile, in a small bowl, drizzle the onion with the remaining 1 tablespoon olive oil, sprinkle with salt and pepper, and toss to coat.

Set a large nonstick grill pan over medium-high heat and let heat for 2 minutes. Add the onion, spreading it in an even layer, and cook, turning occasionally with tongs, until nicely browned on all sides, about 6 minutes. Transfer to a plate and cover to keep warm. Add half of the chicken strips to the pan, spreading them in an even layer, and cook, turning once, until lightly browned on both sides and the meat is opaque throughout when carefully cut into with a knife, about 3 minutes per side. Transfer the chicken to a plate and cover to keep warm. Repeat with the remaining chicken strips and transfer to the plate with the first batch.

Carefully open the pita halves to create pockets. Fill each pocket with lettuce leaf pieces, tomato slices, grilled onion, and grilled chicken, evenly dividing the fillings. Generously drizzle the fillings in each pita with yogurt-tahini sauce and serve right away.

# Smørrebrød

*Smørrebrød* is a Danish open-faced sandwich. The base is a dense sourdough rye bread called *rugbrød*, and it's slathered with softened salted butter and topped with yummy ingredients. If you cannot find *rugbrød*, use a dense whole-grain or rye bread instead.

**MAKES 4 SERVINGS**

**4 slices *rugbrød* or dense, European-style whole-grain or rye bread, whole or cut into your favorite shapes**

**¼ cup (½ stick) salted butter, at room temperature**

**Toppings (see box)**

Spread each slice of bread with 1 tablespoon butter. Top each slice with the toppings of your choice, layering the ingredients in the order listed. Serve right away.

## Ideas for toppings, for each slice of bread

1 small ripe tomato, sliced; and a pinch of chopped fresh chives

1 ounce pickled herring; a few thin slices of red onion; and a pinch of chopped fresh dill

1 ounce sliced smoked salmon; a pinch of chopped fresh dill; and a squeeze of fresh lemon juice

1 ounce sliced roast beef; a few thin slices of red onion; and 1 or 2 cornichons (gherkins), thinly sliced

½ ripe pear, cored and thinly sliced; 1 tablespoon crumbled blue cheese; and 1 tablespoon chopped toasted almonds

½ apple, cored and thinly sliced; 1 tablespoon crumbled goat cheese; and 1 tablespoon chopped cooked bacon

# Tomato Gazpacho

Gazpacho, a cold Spanish soup, is best made in the summertime, when the weather is warm and tomatoes are in season. This recipe uses heirloom tomatoes, which have knockout flavor, but if you can't find them, use very ripe plum tomatoes.

**MAKES 4 SERVINGS**

**2½ pounds ripe red heirloom or plum tomatoes, cored and cut into chunks**

**¾ cup low-sodium tomato juice, plus more as needed**

**3 tablespoons fresh lime juice**

**1 tablespoon red wine vinegar**

**1 red bell pepper, seeded and finely diced**

**⅓ cup finely diced English cucumber**

**1 clove garlic, minced**

**2 tablespoons chopped fresh flat-leaf parsley**

**⅛ teaspoon salt**

Put half of the tomato chunks in a blender and blend until coarsely puréed, about 30 seconds. Pour the purée into a large bowl. Repeat with the remaining tomatoes.

Add the tomato juice, lime juice, vinegar, bell pepper, cucumber, garlic, parsley, and salt and stir gently until well combined. Stir in up to ½ cup more tomato juice to thin the soup, if you like. Cover with plastic wrap and refrigerate until cold, at least 1 hour.

Ladle the chilled soup into bowls and serve.

# Pasta & Bean Soup

The Italian name for this good-for-you soup is *pasta e fagioli,* which means "pasta and beans." It's quick, hearty, and filling—and you might already have all the ingredients to make it in your kitchen!

**MAKES 6 SERVINGS**

3 tablespoons olive oil

1 yellow onion, finely chopped

1 carrot, peeled and finely chopped

1 stalk celery, thinly sliced

1 (14.5-ounce) can diced tomatoes, with juice

8 cups low-sodium beef or chicken broth

1 (15-ounce) can cranberry or cannellini beans, rinsed and drained

2 cups ditalini, tubettini, or other mini pasta shapes

Salt and ground black pepper

Pour the olive oil into a large saucepan and set the pan over medium heat. Add the onion, carrot, and celery and cook, stirring occasionally, until the vegetables are slightly softened, 6 to 8 minutes. Add the tomatoes with their juice, the broth, and the beans to the pan and bring to a boil. Reduce the heat to medium-low and simmer, stirring occasionally, until the vegetables are tender, about 10 minutes.

Raise the heat to medium, add the pasta, and cook, stirring occasionally, until the pasta is al dente (tender but still firm at the center); check the package for the cooking time. Taste the soup (careful, it's hot!) and add as much salt and pepper as you like.

Ladle the soup into bowls and serve right away.

# Tortilla Soup

This traditional Mexican dish is a lot like classic American chicken noodle soup, but crushed tortilla chips replace the noodles. The finished bowls are topped with yummy avocado chunks. If you like, add sour cream and toasted tortilla strips as a garnish too.

**MAKES 4 SERVINGS**

**4 cups low-sodium chicken broth**

**2 cups water**

**2 boneless, skinless chicken breast halves**

**1 carrot, peeled and chopped**

**1 stalk celery, chopped**

**1 clove garlic, thinly sliced**

**½ teaspoon dried thyme, dill, or parsley**

**Salt**

**½ cup tortilla chips, broken into pieces**

**Juice of 1 lime**

**1 ripe avocado, pitted, peeled, and cut into chunks**

**Sour cream, for serving (optional)**

**Toasted tortilla strips, for serving (optional)**

Put the chicken broth and water in a large saucepan. Set the pan over medium heat and bring to a boil. Using tongs, carefully add the chicken breasts to the pan and reduce the heat so that the liquid is simmering gently. Simmer the chicken, uncovered, until cooked through, 10 to 12 minutes. To test if the chicken is done, using tongs, transfer a breast to a plate and carefully cut into it with a small knife; it should be firm and white all the way through. Turn off the heat, transfer the second breast to the plate, and let cool. When the chicken is cool enough to handle, use your fingers or 2 forks to shred it into bite-sized pieces.

Add the carrot, celery, garlic, and thyme to the broth and stir to combine. Bring to a gentle simmer over medium heat and cook until the vegetables are tender, about 10 minutes. Taste the broth and add as much salt as you like. Add the shredded chicken and the tortilla chip pieces, stir to combine, and cook until the chicken is heated through, about 1 minute. Stir in the lime juice.

Ladle the soup into bowls and top each serving with some avocado chunks, a spoonful of sour cream, and toasted tortilla chips, if using. Serve right away.

## Toasted Tortilla Strips

Preheat oven to 450°F. Stack 2 corn tortillas and cut them into ½-inch strips. In a bowl, toss the strips with 1 tablespoon canola oil. Place in a single layer on a cookie sheet and season with salt. Bake until golden brown, about 5 minutes.

# Avocado & Black Bean Tortas

In Mexico, a *torta* is a sandwich, hot or cold, filled with just about any type of ingredients, from scrambled eggs to fried meat cutlets. This version is packed full of fresh, colorful vegetables, and refried black beans spread on the bread help hold it all together.

**MAKES 2 SANDWICHES**

1 cup finely shredded green cabbage

1 ripe tomato, seeded and chopped

2 large radishes, thinly sliced

1 tablespoon fresh lime juice

½ teaspoon hot sauce, such as Sriracha, plus more to taste

2 crusty sandwich rolls, split horizontally

⅔ cup refried black beans, warmed or at room temperature

¼ cup crumbled queso fresco, cotija, or goat cheese

1 small ripe avocado, pitted, peeled, and sliced

Preheat the oven or a toaster oven to 350°F.

In a medium bowl, combine the cabbage, tomato, and radishes. Drizzle with the lime juice and hot sauce and toss until evenly coated. Set aside.

Using your fingers, pull out some of the bread from inside the sandwich roll halves to make space for the fillings. Place the rolls cut sides up on a small cookie sheet and toast in the oven or toaster oven until golden brown, about 5 minutes.

Remove the rolls from the oven. Spread half of the refried beans on the bottom half of each roll. Top with the cheese and avocado slices, dividing them evenly. Mound the cabbage mixture on top of the avocado, dividing it evenly. Cover with the top halves of the rolls and serve right away.

# Cubanos

A Cubano is a small baguette-shaped roll layered with roasted pork, ham, cheese, and pickles and then grilled until warm and crusty. It's a super-deluxe, extra-delicious grilled cheese and a favorite sandwich of anyone who has tasted one!

**MAKES 2 SANDWICHES**

**2 submarine rolls, split**

**1 tablespoon unsalted butter, at room temperature**

**1 tablespoon yellow or Dijon mustard**

**3 ounces Swiss cheese or provolone cheese, thinly sliced**

**2 ounces roasted pork, thinly sliced**

**2 ounces smoked ham, thinly sliced**

**1 dill pickle, thinly sliced**

Spread the crust sides of the rolls with the butter, and then spread the cut sides with the mustard. On the bottom half of each roll, layer one-fourth of the cheese, followed by half of the pork, ham, and pickle slices. Layer the remaining cheese on top, dividing it evenly. Cover with the top halves of the rolls, mustard sides down, and press down gently.

If using a panini press, preheat it. Place the sandwiches in the press, close the top plate, and cook until the bread is golden brown and toasted and the filling is warmed, 3 to 5 minutes.

If cooking on the stovetop, set a medium grill pan or nonstick frying pan over medium heat and let it heat for about 3 minutes. Place the sandwiches in the pan and cook, turning once, until the bread is golden brown and the filling is warmed, 3 to 4 minutes per side. As the sandwiches cook, use a wide metal spatula to press them down once or twice on each side.

Transfer the sandwiches to a cutting board and cut each one in half. Serve right away.

# Matzoh Ball Soup

There are countless family recipes for this classic Jewish comfort food that is often served during Passover in the spring. Seltzer water may seem like an odd ingredient, but its bubbliness helps make the texture of the matzoh balls light and tender.

**MAKES 4 TO 6 SERVINGS**

4 large eggs

3 tablespoons canola oil

1 cup matzoh meal

¼ cup chopped
fresh cilantro

2 tablespoons chopped
flat-leaf parsley

Salt and ground
black pepper

2 tablespoons plain
seltzer water, plus
more as needed

6 cups low-sodium
chicken broth

8 slices peeled ginger

1 leek, white and pale
green parts, chopped

2 tablespoons
minced fresh chives

In a large bowl, whisk the eggs and canola oil until well combined. Add the matzoh meal, cilantro, parsley, ½ teaspoon salt, and ⅛ teaspoon pepper and stir until evenly moistened. Add the seltzer and stir to combine. The mixture should be slightly sticky; if it is too dry, stir in up to 2 additional tablespoons seltzer. Cover the bowl with plastic wrap and refrigerate until cold, about 2 hours.

Fill a large pot three-fourths full of water and add 1 tablespoon salt. Set the pot over high heat and bring the water to a boil. Meanwhile, using your hands, form the chilled matzoh mixture into 1-inch balls; you should have 12 balls. Reduce the heat under the pot so that the water simmers instead of boils. Carefully drop the balls into the water and cook, uncovered, until they rise to the top, 30 to 40 minutes. Using a slotted spoon, transfer the matzoh balls to a large plate. Set aside.

Add the chicken broth and ginger slices to a large saucepan. Set the pan over medium-high heat and bring to a simmer. Reduce the heat to medium-low, add the leek, and cook, uncovered, until the leek is tender, about 10 minutes. Using a slotted spoon, remove and discard the ginger slices. Add the matzoh balls to the simmering broth and cook until heated through, about 3 minutes.

Place 2 to 3 matzoh balls into each soup bowl and ladle in the broth, dividing it evenly. Sprinkle with the chives and serve right away.

PAS

Rice &
Noodles

# Pad Thai

This stir-fried rice noodle dish is a favorite street food in Thailand. The combo of chewy noodles, a tangy-sweet sauce, and crunchy bean sprouts is irresistible wherever you eat it! Tamarind, a sweet-sour fruit, is a traditional ingredient, but ketchup works too.

**MAKES 4 SERVINGS**

**8 ounces dried flat rice noodles**

**3 tablespoons fish sauce**

**1½ tablespoons tamarind or ketchup**

**1 tablespoon sugar**

**2 tablespoons vegetable oil**

**3 garlic cloves, chopped**

**2 large eggs, lightly beaten**

**1 cup bean sprouts**

**3 green onions, thinly sliced**

**1 cup peeled and cooked small shrimp**

**2 tablespoons chopped unsalted roasted peanuts**

**3 tablespoons chopped fresh cilantro**

**Lime wedges, for serving**

Fill a large saucepan three-fourths full of water. Set the pan over high heat and bring the water to a boil. Remove the pan from the heat, add the noodles, and stir well. Let the noodles soften in the water until tender but not mushy, about 5 to 10 minutes. Drain the noodles in a colander set in the sink and set aside.

In a small bowl, combine the fish sauce, tamarind or ketchup, and sugar and stir until the sugar dissolves.

Put the oil in a large frying pan, set the pan over medium heat, and let heat for about 1 minute. Add the garlic and cook, stirring constantly, until golden, about 30 seconds. Add the eggs and cook without stirring until barely set, about 30 seconds. Add the drained noodles and cook, stirring, for 2 minutes. Add ¾ cup of the bean sprouts, half of the green onions, and the shrimp and cook, stirring constantly, until just heated through, 1 to 2 minutes. Pour in the fish sauce mixture and stir to combine.

Transfer the pad thai to a platter. Sprinkle with the remaining bean sprouts and green onions, the peanuts, and the cilantro. Serve right away with lime wedges on the side.

# Japchae

This much-loved Korean dish combines sweet potato noodles, plenty of colorful veggies, and a yummy seasoning mixture of garlic, soy sauce, and a touch of sugar. It's great on its own for lunch, or can be served with grilled or stir-fried steak for a heartier dinner.

**MAKES 4 TO 6 SERVINGS**

**8 to 10 ounces dried Korean sweet potato noodles or cellophane noodles**

**4 teaspoons toasted sesame oil**

**¼ cup low-sodium soy sauce**

**1 tablespoon packed brown sugar**

**1 tablespoon canola oil**

**½ yellow onion, sliced**

**1 large carrot, peeled and cut into matchsticks**

**1 small red bell pepper, seeded and cut into strips**

**Salt and ground black pepper**

**4 ounces fresh shiitake mushrooms, stems removed, caps sliced**

**2 garlic cloves, minced**

**4 ounces baby spinach**

**3 green onions, sliced**

**2 teaspoons sesame seeds**

Fill a large saucepan three-fourths full of water. Set the pan over high heat and bring the water to a boil. Add the noodles, stir well, and cook until tender, about 5 minutes. Drain in a colander set in the sink and rinse under running cold water until cool. Using kitchen shears, cut the noodles into halves or thirds. Drizzle with 2 teaspoons of the sesame oil and toss to coat evenly. Set aside.

In a small bowl, combine the soy sauce, brown sugar, and the remaining 2 teaspoons sesame oil and whisk until the sugar dissolves. Set aside.

Put the canola oil in a large nonstick frying pan. Set the pan over medium heat and let heat for about 1 minute. Add the yellow onion, carrot, and bell pepper, sprinkle with a pinch of salt, and cook, stirring often, until the vegetables have softened slightly, about 5 minutes. Add the mushrooms and garlic and cook, stirring often, until all of the vegetables are tender, about 5 minutes. (Turn down the heat if the vegetables start to brown too quickly.) Add the spinach and toss until wilted. Add the noodles, soy sauce mixture, and green onions, stir, and cook until heated through, about 2 minutes. Taste (careful, it's hot!) and add as much salt and pepper as you like.

Transfer to a platter and sprinkle with the sesame seeds. Serve hot or at room temperature.

# Bucatini all'Amatriciana

This classic Italian dish pairs a spicy tomato sauce with bucatini, a pasta shape that looks like fat spaghetti with a hollow center. *Guanciale* (cured pork cheek) can be hard to find, but you can use pancetta instead. For a milder sauce, use fewer red pepper flakes.

**MAKES 4 TO 6 SERVINGS**

## SAUCE

**2 tablespoons olive oil**

**4 ounces *guanciale* or pancetta, chopped**

**1 small yellow onion, chopped**

**½ teaspoon red pepper flakes**

**3 cloves garlic, minced**

**1 (28-ounce) can crushed tomatoes**

**½ teaspoon dried oregano**

**Salt and ground black pepper**

**16 ounces bucatini or spaghetti**

**2 tablespoons grated pecorino or Parmesan cheese, for serving**

**Chopped parsley, for serving**

To make the sauce, put the olive oil and *guanciale* or pancetta in a large saucepan. Set the pan over medium-high heat and cook, stirring occasionally, until the meat is golden brown and crisp, about 5 minutes. Add the onion and cook, stirring occasionally, until translucent, about 5 minutes. Add the red pepper flakes and garlic and cook until the garlic softens, 1 to 2 minutes. Add the tomatoes, stir to combine, and bring to a boil. Reduce the heat to low, stir in the oregano, and simmer, stirring occasionally, to blend the flavors, about 15 minutes. Taste the sauce (careful, it's hot!) and add as much salt and pepper as you like. Cover to keep warm and set aside.

While the sauce simmers, fill a large pot three-fourths full of water. Set the pot over high heat and bring the water to a boil. Add 1 tablespoon salt and the bucatini, stir well, and cook until the pasta is al dente (tender but still firm at the center); check the package for the cooking time. Drain the pasta in a colander set in the sink and then transfer it to a large serving bowl.

Spoon the sauce over the pasta and, using tongs, toss until evenly coated. Sprinkle the pasta with the cheese and parsley and serve right away.

# Simple Fried Rice

The next time you steam rice, cook enough so that you have leftovers to make fried rice. With eggs and veggies mixed in, it's a complete meal in a bowl. Get creative and swap out any of the ingredients in this basic recipe for your favorite fixings.

**MAKES 4 TO 6 SERVINGS**

2 tablespoons
canola oil

2 cups snow peas,
trimmed and halved
crosswise

4 cups cold cooked
long-grain white rice
(see below)

4 ounces ham steak,
cut into ½-inch cubes

4 green onions, thinly
sliced on the diagonal

2 large eggs, beaten

2 teaspoons toasted
sesame oil

Salt and ground
black pepper

Put 1½ tablespoons of the canola oil in a large nonstick frying pan. Set the pan over medium-high heat and let heat for about 1 minute. Add the snow peas and stir to coat with oil. Carefully sprinkle in about 2 teaspoons water to create steam and cook, stirring often, until the snow peas are slightly softened, 2 to 3 minutes. Add the rice and cook, stirring to break up any clumps, until heated through, about 3 minutes. Stir in the ham and green onions. Using a wooden spoon, make a clearing in the center of the pan. Pour the remaining 1½ teaspoons canola oil into the clearing, and then pour in the eggs. Cook until the eggs are just set, about 1 minute, and then break them up with the wooden spoon. Drizzle the sesame oil over the rice and stir to combine. Turn off the heat. Taste the rice and add as much salt and pepper as you like. Transfer the fried rice to a bowl and serve right away.

## Steamed Rice

Place 2 cups long-grain or short-grain white rice in a large fine-mesh sieve and rinse under running cold water until the water runs clear. Drain well. Transfer the rice to a medium heavy-bottomed saucepan and pour in 3 cups water. Set the pan over medium heat and bring to a boil, stir once, and reduce the heat to low. Cover with a tight-fitting lid and cook, without opening the lid, until the rice is tender and has absorbed all the water, about 15 minutes. Turn off the heat and let sit for 5 minutes. Using a fork, fluff the rice. Serve right away. (If using for fried rice, transfer the rice to an airtight container, let cool uncovered, then cover and refrigerate for up to 4 days.) Makes 4 cups.

# Arroz con Pollo

*Arroz con pollo* means "rice with chicken." This one-pot meal, popular in Spain and Latin America, often includes saffron to give the dish a golden hue and unique flavor. If you can't find saffron, substitute the same amount of ground turmeric, or just leave it out.

**MAKES 4 TO 6 SERVINGS**

**3 pounds bone-in, skin-on chicken thighs, breast halves, and/or drumsticks**

**Salt and ground black pepper**

**3 tablespoons olive oil**

**1 yellow onion, chopped**

**3 jarred roasted red bell peppers, patted dry and cut into ½-inch strips**

**4 large cloves garlic, minced**

**¼ teaspoon saffron threads, crushed with your fingertips, or ¼ teaspoon ground turmeric**

**2 cups long-grain white rice**

**3 cups low-sodium chicken broth**

**2 teaspoons chopped fresh oregano**

**1 (14.5-ounce) can diced tomatoes, with juice**

Preheat the oven to 350°F.

Season the chicken generously on all sides with salt and pepper. Put the oil in a large ovenproof frying pan with a tight-fitting lid. Set the pan over medium-high heat and let heat for 1 minute. Add the chicken in a single layer and cook, turning once or twice with tongs, until golden brown on both sides, about 6 minutes total. Transfer the chicken to a plate. Add the onion, roasted bell peppers, and garlic to the pan, reduce the heat to medium, and cook, stirring occasionally, until the onion has softened, 4 to 5 minutes. Stir the saffron into the vegetables, and then add the rice, stirring to coat the grains. Pour in the chicken broth and add the oregano. Bring to a simmer, stirring occasionally. Return the chicken to the pan, arranging the pieces in a single layer on the rice, and pour in any juices from the plate. Cover the pan, place it in the oven, and cook for 45 minutes.

Carefully remove the pan from the oven. Uncover, add the tomatoes with their juice, and stir to combine. Re-cover and continue to cook in the oven until the rice is tender and most of the liquid is absorbed, about 15 minutes longer. Taste and add as much salt and pepper as you like. Serve right away.

# Couscous with Apricots & Almonds

Couscous, a Moroccan specialty, may look like a grain or seed, but the tiny bits are actually pasta. Serve it as a stand-in for rice with tagines, stews, and grilled meats like Souvlaki (page 46) and Moroccan-Spiced Chicken Skewers (page 47).

### MAKES 6 SERVINGS

⅔ cup slivered almonds

2 cups couscous

2 tablespoons olive oil

⅓ cup dried apricot halves, thinly sliced

2⅔ cups low-sodium chicken broth

½ teaspoon ground turmeric

Salt and ground black pepper

¼ cup dried currants

2 tablespoons fresh lemon juice

1 teaspoon finely grated orange zest

½ cup minced fresh mint (optional)

Preheat the oven to 325°F.

Spread the almonds in a single layer on a small rimmed cookie sheet and toast them in the oven, stirring occasionally, until fragrant and lightly browned, about 10 minutes. (Watch them carefully so that they don't burn!) Remove from the oven and let cool completely.

Put the couscous in a large heatproof bowl, drizzle with the olive oil, and toss until evenly coated. Scatter the apricots over the couscous.

Put the chicken broth in a small saucepan. Set the pan over medium-high heat and bring the broth to a boil. Stir in the turmeric and ¼ teaspoon salt, and then pour the broth over the couscous. Cover the bowl tightly with aluminum foil and let stand until the couscous has absorbed all the liquid, about 5 minutes.

Remove the foil and fluff the couscous with a fork. Stir in the toasted almonds, the currants, lemon juice, orange zest, and mint (if using). Taste and add as much salt and pepper as you like. Mound the couscous in a serving bowl and serve right away.

# Chicken Chow Mein

Stir-fried noodles are popular in China, and the name of this tasty dish means "fried noodles." While the noodles are sometimes served crispy, these are steamed and stay soft. You can find fresh Chinese egg noodles in the refrigerated aisle of the grocery store.

**MAKES 6 SERVINGS**

¼ cup low-sodium soy sauce

¼ cup water

2 teaspoons rice vinegar

1 teaspoon peanut oil

1 teaspoon cornstarch

1 pound fresh Chinese egg noodles

2 tablespoons canola oil

2 boneless, skinless chicken breast halves, sliced crosswise into 2-inch-long strips

8 ounces small shiitake or cremini mushrooms, stems removed, caps quartered

3 heads baby bok choy, cut lengthwise into quarters

1 (15-ounce) can whole baby corn, rinsed and drained

8 ounces snap peas

 In a small bowl, whisk together the soy sauce, water, vinegar, peanut oil, and cornstarch. Set aside.

Fill a large pot three-fourths full of water. Set the pot over high heat and bring the water to a boil. Add the noodles, stir well, and cook until tender; the timing depends on the thickness of the noodles, but you should start checking after about 3 minutes. Drain the noodles in a colander set in the sink.

Put the canola oil in a large frying pan or wok, set the pan over high heat, and let heat for about 1 minute. Add the chicken and cook, stirring often, until browned, about 5 minutes. Transfer to a large plate. Add the mushrooms, bok choy, baby corn, and snap peas to the pan. Cook, stirring constantly, until the veggies are tender, about 5 minutes. Stir the soy sauce mixture to recombine, then pour it over the veggies. Cook, stirring constantly, until the sauce is bubbling and thickened, about 2 minutes. Return the chicken to the pan, add the noodles, and toss to combine.

Transfer the chow mein to a platter or large bowl and serve right away.

# Hawaiian Fried Rice

This yummy fried rice features ham, pineapple, and ginger, for a flavor combo that's savory, sweet-tart, and mildly spicy. Look for peeled and cored fresh pineapple in the produce area of the market, and use low-sodium soy sauce or the dish will be too salty.

**MAKES 4 TO 6 SERVINGS**

¼ cup low-sodium soy sauce

1 teaspoon toasted sesame oil

1 teaspoon Sriracha hot sauce, or to taste (optional)

2½ tablespoons canola oil

1 red bell pepper, seeded and chopped

12 ounces ham steak, cut into ½-inch cubes

1 heaping cup fresh pineapple cut into ½-inch chunks

4 green onions, thinly sliced on the diagonal

3 garlic cloves, minced

1 tablespoon peeled and grated fresh ginger

4 cups cold cooked long-grain white rice (see Steamed Rice, page 83)

2 large eggs, beaten

 In a small bowl, whisk together the soy sauce, sesame oil, and hot sauce (if using). Set aside.

Put 1 tablespoon of the canola oil in a large nonstick frying pan. Set the pan over medium-high heat and let heat for about 1 minute. Add the bell pepper and ham and cook, stirring often, until the pepper is slightly softened, about 6 minutes. Add the pineapple, green onions, garlic, and ginger and cook, stirring often, until fragrant, about 4 minutes. Transfer to a bowl and set aside.

Add 1 tablespoon canola oil to the frying pan. Set the pan over medium-high heat and let heat for 1 minute. Add the rice and cook, stirring to break up any clumps, until heated through, about 3 minutes. Using a wooden spoon, make a clearing in the center of the pan by pushing the rice to the sides. Pour the remaining 1½ teaspoons canola oil into the clearing, and then pour in the eggs. Cook until the eggs are just set, about 1 minute, and then break them up with the wooden spoon and mix them into the rice. Pour in the soy sauce mixture and stir to combine. Return the ham mixture to the pan and cook, stirring constantly, until the rice has absorbed the liquid, about 2 minutes.

Transfer the fried rice to a bowl and serve right away.

**Hot stuff**
To check if an empty pan (one without any oil) is hot enough before adding food, toss a drop of water into it; if it sizzles, the pan is ready.

# Chicken, Broccoli & Cashew Stir-Fry

This is a super-tasty one-pan meal that you can make in just minutes. Once you start stir-frying, the cooking process goes very quickly, so make sure you have all of the ingredients prepped and ready to go near the stove. Serve it with steamed rice (page 83).

**MAKES 4 TO 6 SERVINGS**

Salt and ground black pepper

1½ cups broccoli florets

2 tablespoons low-sodium soy sauce

2 teaspoons rice vinegar

1 teaspoon cornstarch

1 pound boneless, skinless chicken breast halves, cut into ½-inch cubes

¼ cup low-sodium chicken broth

2 tablespoons oyster sauce

2 tablespoons peeled and minced fresh ginger

2 cloves garlic, minced

¼ cup roasted cashews

Hot sauce, such as Sriracha, for serving (optional)

Fill a medium saucepan three-fourths full of water. Set the pan over high heat and bring the water to a boil. Add 1 teaspoon salt and the broccoli and cook until tender-crisp, about 3 minutes. Drain in a colander set in the sink and set aside.

In a large bowl, whisk together 1 tablespoon of the soy sauce, the vinegar, ½ teaspoon of the cornstarch, ¼ teaspoon salt, and ¼ teaspoon pepper. Add the chicken and toss to coat. Let stand at room temperature for 10 minutes.

In a small bowl, whisk together the chicken broth, oyster sauce, the remaining 1 tablespoon soy sauce, and the remaining ½ teaspoon cornstarch. Set aside near the stove.

Set a large nonstick frying pan or wok over high heat and let heat for about 2 minutes. Add the chicken and its marinade and cook, stirring often, until the chicken is opaque throughout, about 6 minutes. Add the ginger and garlic and cook, stirring constantly, until the mixture is fragrant, about 30 seconds. Stir the broth mixture to recombine, and then pour it into the pan. Cook, stirring constantly, until the sauce is bubbling and thickened, about 2 minutes. Add the cashews and broccoli and stir to combine. Serve right away, with hot sauce, if you like.

# Vegetable Paella

Traditional Spanish paella combines rice with meat and/or seafood, but this version is packed with colorful veggies. Stubby medium-grain rice, which has a creamy texture when cooked, is key. Look for Bomba rice from Spain, but Arborio rice from Italy works too.

**MAKES 6 SERVINGS**

¼ cup olive oil

1 green bell pepper, seeded and cut into 1½-inch pieces

1 cup broccoli florets

1 cup cauliflower florets

1 cup frozen peeled fava beans, thawed

5 ounces green beans, trimmed and cut into 2-inch pieces

3 cloves garlic, thinly sliced

1 cup frozen peas, thawed

1¼ cups canned tomato purée

9 cups low-sodium vegetable broth

1 tablespoon salt

2 cups Bomba or Arborio rice

Lemon wedges, for serving

Pour the olive oil into a 15-inch paella pan or large sauté pan with sides 2 inches high. Set the pan over medium-high heat and let heat for 1 minute. Add the bell pepper, broccoli, cauliflower, fava beans, and green beans and cook, stirring occasionally, until the veggies are lightly browned, about 5 minutes. Add the garlic and peas and cook, stirring constantly, for 30 seconds. Add the tomato purée, vegetable broth, and salt and stir to combine. Bring to a simmer and add the rice, stirring to mix the grains into the veggies. Reduce the heat to low and simmer uncovered without stirring until the rice has absorbed almost all of the liquid and is a little more tender than al dente, about 20 minutes.

Remove the pan from the heat, cover with aluminum foil or the lid, and let stand for 5 to 10 minutes (during this time the rice will absorb any remaining liquid). Bring the pan to the table (make sure to set it on a trivet) and serve with the lemon wedges on the side.

PAS
NEW ZEALAND
03•12
SOUTH
10•11
AFRICA
03•08
ISRAEL
04•01
THE UNITED
KINGDOM
FRANCE
12•12
05•06
GERMANY

Drinks &
Desserts

# Mexican Chocolate Pudding

Once you've tasted homemade chocolate pudding—and discovered how simple it is to make—you'll never make the instant kind again. This version, inspired by Mexican chocolate, is flavored with cinnamon and a hint of heat from cayenne pepper.

**MAKES 4 SERVINGS**

¼ cup firmly packed light brown sugar

2 tablespoons cornstarch

½ teaspoon ground cinnamon

⅛ teaspoon cayenne pepper (optional)

⅛ teaspoon salt

2 cups whole milk

2 large egg yolks

4 ounces bittersweet chocolate, finely chopped

½ teaspoon vanilla extract

Whipped cream (see page 104), for serving

Chocolate sprinkles, for serving

 In a small bowl, stir together the brown sugar, cornstarch, cinnamon, cayenne (if using), and salt. Set aside.

In a medium saucepan, whisk together the milk and egg yolks. Add the brown sugar mixture and whisk well. Set the pan over medium heat and cook, stirring constantly with a heatproof rubber spatula or a wooden spoon until the sugar is dissolved and the mixture begins to bubble, about 5 minutes. Continue to cook, stirring constantly, for 1 minute longer, and then remove the pan from the heat. Add the chocolate and stir until melted and smooth, and then stir in the vanilla.

Divide the pudding evenly among 4 ramekins or serving bowls and smooth the tops. Place a piece of waxed paper directly on the surface of each portion to prevent a skin from forming. Refrigerate for at least 2 hours or up to 3 days.

To serve, top each pudding with a dollop of whipped cream and chocolate sprinkles. Serve cold.

# Hawaiian Shave Ice

Shave ice is a beloved treat in Hawaii. To make it, vendors shave large blocks of ice to a light, fluffy texture using a special machine, and then the mound of ice is drizzled with fruit-flavored syrups. You can make a similar treat at home by crushing ice in a blender.

**MAKES 2 SERVINGS**

**STRAWBERRY SYRUP**

**1 (1-pound) bag frozen strawberries, thawed and chopped**

**1 cup water**

**½ cup sugar**

**3 cups ice cubes**

**Vanilla ice cream (optional)**

To make the strawberry syrup, combine the strawberries, water, and sugar in a medium saucepan. Set the pan over medium-high heat and bring the mixture to a boil, stirring occasionally. Reduce the heat to medium and simmer gently until the strawberries lose their color and the syrup is bright red, about 7 minutes. Set a fine-mesh sieve over a bowl, pour in the strawberry mixture, and strain the liquid (do not press on the solids). Discard the solids in the sieve. Let the syrup cool to room temperature, transfer to an airtight container, and refrigerate until cold, at least 1 hour. (You should have about 1½ cups syrup; it will keep in the refrigerator for up to 1 week.)

Put the ice in a blender and pulse to blend on medium-high speed until the ice is very fine; discard any large bits that remain. If you like, put 1 small scoop of vanilla ice cream into each of 2 short drinking glasses or paper cones. Scoop in the crushed ice, dividing it evenly, and drizzle with a few tablespoons of the syrup. Serve right away.

## Pineapple and Mango Variations

Combine 1 cup pure unsweetened pineapple or mango juice, ½ cup sugar, and ¼ cup water in a medium saucepan. Set the pan over medium-high heat, bring to a boil, and cook, stirring occasionally, for 2 minutes. Let cool to room temperature, transfer to an airtight container, and refrigerate until cold, at least 1 hour. Makes about 1¼ cups.

# Kiwi & Berry Pavlovas

This fun dessert from New Zealand is named after Anna Pavlova, a Russian ballerina. It's a crisp meringue topped with lots of fluffy whipped cream and colorful fresh fruit. (Meringue is a mixture of egg whites and sugar that is beaten until it's light and airy.)

**MAKES 6 TO 8 SERVINGS**

**MERINGUES**

**Nonstick cooking spray**

**4 large egg whites**

**Pinch of salt**

**1 cup sugar**

**1 teaspoon cornstarch**

**½ teaspoon white vinegar**

**WHIPPED CREAM**

**1 cup heavy cream**

**2 tablespoons sugar**

**½ teaspoon vanilla extract**

**3 kiwis, peeled and thinly sliced**

**2 cups raspberries**

**1 cup blueberries**

 Preheat the oven to 325°F. Lightly spray a cookie sheet with nonstick cooking spray and line it with parchment paper.

To make the meringues, in the bowl of a stand mixer, combine the egg whites and salt. Whip with the whisk attachment on high speed until foamy, about 1 minute. With the mixer running, slowly add the sugar and continue to whip until the whites hold stiff, glossy peaks when the whisk attachment is lifted, about 10 minutes. Add the cornstarch and vinegar and whip on medium speed just until combined.

If you'd like to make 1 large pavlova, spoon the meringue onto the center of the prepared cookie sheet. Use the back of a spoon to spread it into a 9-inch round and create an indentation in the center of the round, leaving a 1-inch border around the edge. If you'd like to make individual pavlovas, spoon 6 to 8 mounds of the meringue onto the prepared sheet, dividing it evenly and spacing the mounds evenly apart. Spread each mound into a 3- to 4-inch round, and then use the back of the spoon to create an indentation in the center of each round.

Bake for 2 minutes, and then reduce the oven temperature to 250°F. Continue to bake until dry to the touch, about 1 hour for individual meringues or 1¾ hours for a large meringue. Turn off the oven and leave the meringue(s) in the oven to dry and cool completely, at least 2 hours or up to overnight.

To make the whipped cream, in the bowl of the stand mixer, combine the cream, sugar, and vanilla. Whip with the whisk attachment on low speed until slightly thickened, 1 to 2 minutes. Gradually increase the speed to medium-high and continue to whip until the cream holds medium-stiff peaks when the whisk attachment is lifted, 3 to 4 minutes longer. Take care not to overwhip the cream.

To serve, if you've made 1 large meringue, place it on a platter; if you've made individual meringues, place each one on a serving plate. Fill the center(s) with the whipped cream, dividing it evenly if serving individual pavlovas. Top with the kiwi slices, raspberries, and blueberries and serve right away.

# Pineapple-Coconut Smoothie

One sip of this delicious drink and you'll feel like you're on a tropical beach. Kaffir lime leaves, an ingredient used in Thai cooking, have a bold lime flavor. Look for them in specialty grocery stores or Asian markets, or use 2 teaspoons of fresh lime zest instead.

**MAKES 3 SERVINGS**

**1 ripe pineapple, peeled, cored, and cut into chunks, or 3 cups frozen pineapple chunks**

**1 (14-ounce) can coconut milk**

**4 kaffir lime leaves or 2 teaspoons fresh lime zest**

**Ice cubes, for serving**

Put the pineapple chunks, coconut milk, and kaffir lime leaves in a blender and blend until smooth, about 2 minutes.

Fill 3 glasses with ice cubes, pour in the fruit mixture, and serve right away.

### Crazy for coconut

*Add a scoop of coconut ice cream to the blender for a really dreamy dessert drink!*

# Black Forest Cake

In this majestic German dessert, chocolate cake layers are filled with cherry-studded whipped cream and topped with more whipped cream. You can make the cake layers a day ahead, wrap them well in plastic wrap, and store them at room temperature.

**MAKES 8 TO 10 SERVINGS**

**CAKE**

½ cup cake flour

½ cup unsweetened Dutch-process cocoa powder

½ cup (1 stick) unsalted butter, melted and cooled

6 large eggs

¾ cup granulated sugar

1½ teaspoons vanilla extract

½ teaspoon salt

1 (24-ounce) jar pitted red sour cherries in light syrup

2 cups heavy cream

2 tablespoons powdered sugar

1½ teaspoons vanilla extract

1 cup chocolate sprinkles

To make the cake, preheat the oven to 350°F. Line the bottoms of two 9-inch round cake pans with parchment paper rounds. (Place each cake pan on a piece of parchment paper, trace around the bottom with a pencil, and then use scissors to cut out the circle, cutting just inside of the pencil line.)

Sift the flour and cocoa powder into a bowl. Put the melted butter in a medium bowl. In a large bowl, using an electric mixer, beat the eggs, granulated sugar, vanilla, and salt on high speed until light and fluffy, about 5 minutes. Sprinkle the flour mixture over the egg mixture and, using a large rubber spatula, gently fold just until combined. Stir a big spoonful of the batter into the melted butter until well blended, and then add this mixture back into the batter and gently fold with the spatula until well combined. Divide the batter evenly between the prepared pans.

Bake the cakes until a wooden skewer inserted into the center comes out clean, about 20 minutes. Remove from the oven and let cool in the pans on a wire rack for about 20 minutes.

One cake at a time, slide a paring knife between the edge of the cake and the sides of the pan to loosen and carefully invert the cake onto the rack. Lift off the cake pan, peel off the parchment round, and let cool completely.

Set a fine-mesh sieve over a bowl and drain the cherries, reserving the juice.

~ *Continued on page 112* ~

**Cherry-licious!**

*Save leftover cherries from this recipe for oatmeal and boil down their juice to make a syrup for sparkling water.*

~ *Continued from page 111* ~

Set aside 13 of the prettiest cherries in a small bowl. Measure out 1 cup of drained cherries and put them in a medium bowl.

In a large bowl, using an electric mixer, beat the cream, powdered sugar, and vanilla on low speed until slightly thickened, 1 to 2 minutes. Gradually increase the speed to medium-high and continue to beat until the cream holds medium-stiff peaks when the beaters are lifted, 3 to 4 minutes longer. Take care not to overwhip the cream.

To assemble the cake, very carefully place one cake layer on a cake platter or cake stand. Add 1 cup of the whipped cream to the cherries in the bowl and gently fold together to combine. Spread this mixture on top of the first cake layer. Carefully place the second cake layer on top, lining up the layers. If you like, fit a pastry bag with a star tip and put about ½ cup of the whipped cream in the bag; set the bag aside. Using an icing spatula, spread the remaining whipped cream all over the top and sides of the cake, smoothing the surfaces as best you can.

Cover the top and sides of the cake with the chocolate sprinkles. If you saved whipped cream in a pastry bag, twist the wide end of the bag to push the cream to the tip and pipe 12 rosettes (rose-shaped decorations that are made with the star tip of a piping bag) on top of the cake, evenly spaced around the edge, and 1 in the center. Place 1 cherry in each rosette. (If you are not piping rosettes, place 12 of the reserved cherries on top of the cake, evenly spaced around the edge, and 1 in the center.) Serve right away or refrigerate for up to 2 hours.

# Chai Milkshake

*Chai* is the word for "tea" in India, and it is often brewed with sweetened hot milk and a mixture of good-smelling spices. Black peppercorns might seem like a weird addition to a drink, but their flavor goes really well with the other spices in the mix.

**MAKES 4 SERVINGS**

4 cups whole milk

2 tablespoons sugar

4 chai tea bags

10 black peppercorns

3 thin slices peeled fresh ginger

1 pint vanilla ice cream, slightly softened

Whipped cream (see page 104), for serving (optional)

Ground cinnamon, for serving (optional)

Combine the milk and sugar in a medium saucepan. Set the pan over medium-high heat and heat the milk, stirring to dissolve the sugar, until steam begins to rise. Remove from the heat and add the tea bags, peppercorns, and ginger. Steep for 5 minutes, then remove the tea bags. Let cool to room temperature.

Transfer the mixture to a container, cover, and refrigerate until cold, at least 2 hours or up to overnight. (To chill the chai quickly, transfer it from the saucepan to a bowl and nest it in a larger bowl filled with ice.)

Set a fine-mesh sieve across the top of a blender and strain the chai into the blender. Add the ice cream and blend until smooth. Divide the milkshake evenly among 4 glasses. Top with dollops of whipped cream and sprinkle with cinnamon, if using, and serve right away.

# Tres Leches Cakes

*Tres leches* means "three milks" in Spanish. This favorite Latin American treat gets its name because a trio of sweetened condensed, evaporated, and whole milk is used to soak the cake after baking so that it's incredibly moist and delicious.

**MAKES 12 SERVINGS**

## CAKES

**Unsalted butter, for greasing the pan**

**1 (12-ounce) can sweetened condensed milk**

**1 (12-ounce) can evaporated milk**

**1 cup heavy cream**

**1 cup all-purpose flour**

**¾ cup granulated sugar**

**1 teaspoon baking powder**

**¼ teaspoon salt**

**3 large eggs, at room temperature**

**½ cup whole milk**

**1 teaspoon vanilla extract**

**Whipped cream (see page 104), for serving**

Preheat the oven to 350°F. Butter a standard 12-cup muffin pan.

To make the cakes, in a 9-by-13-inch glass baking dish, stir together the sweetened condensed milk, evaporated milk, and heavy cream until well combined and set aside. In a large bowl, whisk together the flour, granulated sugar, baking powder, and salt. In a medium bowl, whisk the eggs, milk, and vanilla until well combined. Pour the egg mixture into the flour mixture and whisk gently just until the batter is evenly moistened.

Divide the batter evenly among the prepared muffin cups. Bake until the cakes are light golden brown and a wooden skewer inserted in the center of a cake comes out clean, 18 to 20 minutes. Remove from the oven and poke each cake several times with the skewer. While the cakes are still hot, carefully invert them onto a wire rack to remove them from the pan, and place them in a single layer in the baking dish with the milk and cream mixture. Generously spoon the milk and cream mixture over each cake. Let the soaked cakes cool completely in the baking dish, about 1 hour.

Carefully transfer the cakes to an airtight container, arranging them in a single layer, and cover tightly. Pour the soaking mixture into a separate container and cover tightly. Refrigerate both the cakes and the soaking mixture for at least 4 hours or up to 2 days, spooning more soaking mixture over the cakes from time to time to keep them moist.

~ *Continued on page 118* ~

## Baking game plan

*Start preparing these cakes in the morning since they need a few hours to soak up all of the sweet milky sauce.*

～ *Continued from page 117* ～

Before serving, let the cakes stand at room temperature for about 10 minutes.

Put the cakes in individual bowls and spoon a few tablespoons of the soaking liquid on top so that it pools in the bowl. Dollop each with whipped cream and serve right away.

# Sticky Toffee Pudding

In Britain, desserts of any kind are called "puddings." Sweet, gooey dates are the star of this popular "pudding," which is actually a moist, tender cake. You can top each cake with a big scoop of vanilla ice cream before drizzling on the toffee sauce, if you like.

**MAKES 8 SERVINGS**

½ cup finely chopped pitted dates

¾ teaspoon baking soda

¾ cup boiling water

1 cup all-purpose flour, plus more for dusting

1¼ teaspoons baking powder

½ teaspoon salt

¼ cup (½ stick) unsalted butter, at room temperature, plus more for greasing

¾ cup brown sugar

2 large eggs

2 teaspoons vanilla extract

**SAUCE**

¼ cup (½ stick) unsalted butter

¾ cup dark brown sugar

¾ cup heavy cream

2 teaspoons vanilla extract

Pinch of salt

 Preheat the oven to 350°F. Butter eight ½-cup custard cups or ramekins and dust them with flour, turning and tapping to coat evenly. Place the custard cups on a rimmed cookie sheet.

To make the cakes, in a small heatproof bowl, combine the dates and baking soda and pour in the boiling water. Let stand until cooled. In a small bowl, whisk together the flour, baking powder, and salt.

In a large bowl using an electric mixer or stand mixer fitted with the paddle attachment, beat the butter and brown sugar on medium speed until lightened, about 3 minutes. Add the eggs one at a time, beating well after each addition. Add the vanilla and beat until combined. Add the flour mixture and mix on low speed until evenly moistened. Add the date mixture and mix on low speed until well combined. The batter will be thin.

Divide the batter evenly among the prepared custard cups. Bake until the cakes are puffed and a wooden skewer inserted into the center comes out clean, about 20 minutes.

To make the toffee sauce, melt the butter in a small saucepan set over medium heat. Add the brown sugar and cream and whisk until the sugar dissolves and the sauce is sticky, about 5 minutes. Whisk in the vanilla and salt.

To serve, turn each warm cake out of the custard cup onto an individual serving plate. Spoon on some toffee sauce and serve right away.

# Watermelon-Lime Refresher

This pretty-in-pink Latin-style fruit drink is perfect for cooling off on hot summer days. Serve a large pitcher of it at an outdoor party paired with flavorful dishes like Tex-Mex Chicken and Black Bean Nachos (page 24) or Beef Empanadas (page 38).

**MAKES 4 SERVINGS**

**Zest and juice of 2 limes**

**6 cups seedless watermelon chunks**

**2 teaspoons honey**

**¼ cup water**

**Ice cubes, for serving**

**Club soda, for serving**

**Lime slices and diced seedless watermelon, for garnish**

Finely grate the lime zest and set aside.

Put the watermelon chunks, lime juice, honey, and water in a blender and blend until smooth, about 1 minute.

Fill a large pitcher with ice cubes. Pour in the watermelon-lime juice and add club soda to fill the pitcher. Stir in the lime zest, garnish with the lime slices and diced watermelon, and serve right away.

# Krembo

Krembo, a popular Israeli confection, is a cookie base topped with marshmallowy meringue and then dipped in chocolate. Allow enough time to make this dessert, and use a candy thermometer to check the temperature of the sugar syrup for the meringue.

**MAKES ABOUT 56 COOKIES**

**COOKIE BASE**

¾ cup (1½ sticks) unsalted butter, at room temperature

⅔ cup sugar

½ teaspoon salt

1 large egg yolk

1 teaspoon vanilla extract

1½ cups all-purpose flour, plus more for dusting

**MERINGUE**

4 large egg whites

½ teaspoon cream of tartar

1 cup sugar

1 tablespoon light corn syrup or lemon juice

¼ cup water

**CHOCOLATE COATING**

16 ounces semisweet chocolate chips

3 tablespoons canola oil

To make the cookie base, in a large bowl, using an electric mixer, beat the butter, sugar, and salt on medium speed until well combined, about 2 minutes. Add the egg yolk and vanilla and beat until combined. Add the flour and beat on low speed until the mixture is evenly moistened and starts to come together in clumps. Lightly flour a clean work surface. Dump the dough onto the surface and press it together with your hands. Divide the dough in half and form each mound into a ball. Shape each ball into a log about 1¼ inches in diameter and about 10 inches long. Wrap each log tightly in plastic wrap and refrigerate until well chilled, at least 1 hour or up to overnight.

To bake the cookies, position 2 racks so they are evenly spaced in the oven and preheat the oven to 375°F. Line 2 cookie sheets with parchment paper.

Unwrap the dough logs and slice them into rounds just shy of ½ inch thick. Arrange the rounds on the prepared cookie sheets, spacing them about 1 inch apart. Bake for about 7 minutes. Using oven mitts, rotate the cookie sheets from top to bottom and front to back and continue to bake until they are light golden brown around the edges, about 8 minutes longer. Remove from the oven and let cool on the cookie sheets on wire racks. Combine all of the cookies onto 1 cookie sheet, arranging them in a single layer.

To make the meringue, in the bowl of a stand mixer fitted with the whisk attachment, combine the egg whites and cream of tartar. Put the sugar, corn syrup or lemon juice, and water in a small, heavy-bottomed saucepan and clip a candy thermometer to the side of the pan. Set the pan over medium-high heat and bring to a boil, occasionally swirling the pan (don't stir the contents). When the syrup reaches a boil, whip the egg whites on medium speed until they hold medium-stiff peaks when the whisk attachment is lifted, about 2 minutes. Take care not to overbeat them. Continue to boil the syrup, swirling the pan from time to time, until the sugar syrup registers 240°F on the candy thermometer. Remove the pan from the heat. Ask an adult to help you with the next step and work quickly. With the mixer running on medium-low speed, very carefully drizzle the hot sugar syrup into the egg whites. After you've added all of the sugar syrup, increase the speed to medium-high and whip the whites until the outside of the bowl is cool to the touch and the meringue is stiff and glossy, about 5 minutes.

Fit a large pastry bag with a ¼-inch plain tip. Scrape about half of the meringue into the bag and twist the wide end of the bag to push the meringue to the tip. Pipe a 1½- to 2-inch-high mound of meringue onto each cookie, swirling to create a point at the top. Refill the pastry bag when needed. Place the cookie sheet in the freezer and let chill for about 1 hour to firm up the meringue.

To make the chocolate coating, put the chocolate chips in a microwave-safe bowl. Microwave on high heat, stirring every 30 seconds, until melted and smooth. Add the oil and stir until well combined.

Remove the meringue-topped cookies from the freezer. Holding a cookie by its base, turn it upside down and dip just the meringue into the chocolate; use a spoon to drizzle the chocolate onto any uncoated spots so that the meringue is completely covered. Turn the cookie upright and set it on a wire rack. Repeat to coat all of the cookies. (If the chocolate hardens, microwave it for a few seconds.)

Let stand at room temperature for about 1 hour, or until the chocolate sets.

# Mango Lassi

Lassi is an Indian yogurt drink. The sweet fruitiness and cool creaminess of a mango lassi are perfect for balancing fiery, highly spiced Indian dishes. But it's also great for breakfast, as an after-school snack, or even for dessert.

**MAKES 4 SERVINGS**

**2 ripe mangoes, peeled, pitted, and cut into cubes, or 2 cups pre-cut fresh mango slices**

**1 teaspoon fresh lemon juice**

**2 tablespoons sugar or honey, plus more as needed**

**2 cups plain yogurt**

**1 cup ice cubes**

In a blender, combine the mangoes, lemon juice, sugar or honey, yogurt, and ice cubes. Blend until frothy and smooth. Taste and add more sugar or honey, if you like.

Divide the lassi evenly among 4 tall glasses and serve right away.

**Speedy shortcut**
*Use 2 cups frozen mango chunks instead of fresh mango slices, and skip the ice cubes.*

# "Marshmallow" Pudding

Don't let the name fool you. This South African baked pudding, which is actually a cake, doesn't contain any marshmallows, but its spongy texture feels like the sugary treats. To make mini versions, use a 12-cup muffin pan and bake for about 15 to 20 minutes.

**MAKES 6 SERVINGS**

## CAKES

Unsalted butter, for greasing the pan

1¼ cups all-purpose flour

1 teaspoon baking soda

½ teaspoon salt

2 large eggs

⅔ cup sugar

2 tablespoons unsalted butter, melted

2 tablespoons apricot jam

1 teaspoon white vinegar

½ cup whole milk

## SAUCE

½ cup (1 stick) unsalted butter

¾ cup heavy cream

½ cup fresh orange juice

½ cup sugar

Pinch of salt

1 teaspoon vanilla extract

 To make the cakes, preheat the oven to 350°F. Butter six 1-cup ramekins and place them on a rimmed cookie sheet.

In a medium bowl, whisk together the flour, baking soda, and salt.

In a large bowl, using an electric mixer, beat the eggs and sugar on medium speed until light and fluffy, about 4 minutes. Beat in the melted butter, apricot jam, and vinegar. Add about one-third of the flour mixture and mix on low speed until barely combined. Pour in half of the milk and beat on low just until combined. Beat in half of the remaining flour mixture, then the remaining milk, and finally the remaining flour, and mix until the batter is moistened.

Divide the batter evenly among the prepared ramekins; they should be no more than two-thirds full. Bake until golden brown and a toothpick inserted into the center of a cake comes out clean, about 30 minutes.

While the cakes bake, to make the sauce, melt the butter in a medium saucepan set over medium-low heat. Add the cream, orange juice, sugar, and salt. Simmer, stirring occasionally, until the sugar is dissolved, about 3 minutes. Do not let the sauce boil. Remove from the heat, stir in the vanilla, and cover.

When the cakes are done, remove them from the oven and set the baking sheet on a wire rack. Immediately pierce the cakes all over with a wooden skewer. Pour some of the warm sauce over each cake. Serve the puddings warm or at room temperature, with the remaining sauce alongside.

# French Apple Tart

Impress your friends with this dessert that looks super fancy but uses only four ingredients and is super easy to make! The secret: frozen puff pastry, which you roll into a big rectangle before layering on the sliced apples.

**MAKES 6 TO 8 SERVINGS**

**All-purpose flour, for dusting**

**1 sheet frozen puff pastry, thawed overnight in the refrigerator**

**2 Granny Smith, Braeburn, Fuji, or Cortland apples**

**¼ cup sugar**

 Preheat the oven to 425°F. Line a rimmed cookie sheet with parchment paper.

Very lightly dust a clean work surface with flour. Lay the puff pastry on the surface and lightly dust the top with flour. Using a rolling pin, roll out the sheet to a 10-by-15-inch rectangle about ⅛ inch thick. Place the rectangle on the prepared cookie sheet and put in the freezer to chill while you prepare the apples.

Core the apples with an apple corer or paring knife and cut them in half lengthwise. Slice each half into ¼-inch-thick half-moons.

Remove the pastry from the freezer. With a sharp paring knife, cut a 1-inch border along the edges of the puff pastry, being careful not to cut more than halfway through the pastry. Prick the pastry inside of the border all over with a fork, and then sprinkle evenly with 2 tablespoons of the sugar. Arrange the apple slices in slightly overlapping rows on the pastry inside of the border and sprinkle the apples evenly with the remaining 2 tablespoons sugar.

Bake until the pastry is golden brown and the apples are tender, 15 to 20 minutes. Remove from the oven and let cool on the cookie sheet on a wire rack. Cut into pieces and serve warm or at room temperature.

# Index

# weldon**owen**

1150 Brickyard Cove Road, Richmond, CA 94801
weldonowen.com

WELDON OWEN INTERNATIONAL
President & Publisher  Roger Shaw
SVP, Sales & Marketing  Amy Kaneko

Associate Publisher  Amy Marr
Project Editor  Alexis Mersel

Creative Director  Kelly Booth
Associate Art Director  Lisa Berman
Original Design  Alexandra Zeigler

Production Director  Michelle Duggan
Production Manager  Sam Bissell
Production Designer  Howie Severson
Imaging Manager  Don Hill

Photographer  Nicole Hill Gerulat
Food Stylists  Marion Cooper Cairns, Lillian Kang
Wardrobe & Prop Stylists  Veronica Olson, Ethel Brennan
Hair & Makeup  Nina Fife
Passport Stamp Illustrator  Conor Buckley

AMERICAN GIRL *AROUND THE WORLD*
Conceived and produced by Weldon Owen International
In collaboration with Williams Sonoma, Inc.
3250 Van Ness Avenue, San Francisco, CA 94109

Printed and bound in China

First printed in 2017
10 9 8 7 6 5

Library of Congress Cataloging in Publication
data is available

ISBN: 978-1-68188-280-2

ACKNOWLEDGMENTS
Weldon Owen wishes to thank the following people for their generous support to help produce this
book: Erica Allen, Lesley Bruynesteyn, Jean Erikson, Nina & Dan Fife, Lexi Hager, Bonnie Hughes, Kim Laidlaw,
Veronica Laramie, Rachel Markowitz, David Marks, Hristina Misafiris, A'Lissa Olson,
Taylor Olson, Monika Ottehenning, Elizabeth Parson, Tamara White, and Dawn Yanagihara

A VERY SPECIAL THANK YOU TO:
Our models: Kayli Count, Alexa Fo, DeShawn Hoy, Jianna Kumar, Hannah Lowe, Maeve Mansfield, Jillian Rose Metzger,
Theia Minev, Alyssa Rivera, Sasha Whitman, Magnus Warmsley, Leah Wharton, Olivia Zuker-Brunzell

Our locations: Nina & Dan Fife, The Snyder Family
Our party resources: Sarah Morrison/Paper Built, Rice by Rice, Stesha Party